LIST OF HIKES IN THIS BOOK

1) South Rim
2) Apache Canyon
3) The Window
4) Lost Mine
5) Juniper Canyon
6) Dodson Ranch
7) Boquillas Canyon
8) Mule Ears Spring
9) Tornillo Creek
10) Burro Mesa Pouroff
11) Burro Springs
12) Red Rocks
13) The Chimneys
14) Santa Elena Canyon
15) North Ridge
16) Tall Grass
17) Hospital Canyon

18) Monahans Sandhills
19) Guadalupe Mountains
20) McKittrick Canyon
21) Palo Duro Canyon
22) Lake Texoma
23) Caprock/Greer Island
24) Crosstimbers
25) Little Springs/Forest
26) Bosque Trail
27) Dinosaur Valley
28) LBJ State Park
29) Pedernales Park
30) Palmetto
31) Padre Island
32) Aransas Refuge
33) Kirby Primitive/Old Carter
34) Moscow/Bull Creek

35) Longleaf Pine/Dogwood
36) Old River/Griff Ross
37) Huntsville Park
38) Mission Tejas
39) Caddo Lake/Daingerfield
40) Ratcliff Trail
41) Big Slough Trail
42) Four-C's
43) Lone Star Trail
44) Little Lake Creek Loop
45) Stubblefield Lake
46) Four Notch Loop
47) Double Lake
48) Mercy Trail
49) Big Creek Scenic Area
50) Winter's Bayou

50 HIKES IN TEXAS

Texas Madrone in McKittrick Canyon

50 HIKES IN TEXAS

REVISED EDITION

BY HARRY EVANS

50 HIKES IN TEXAS

Gem Guides Book Co.
3677 San Gabriel River Parkway
Pico Rivera, CA 90660

**Photo on cover: View from the South Rim,
Big Bend National Park**

INTRODUCTION

Everyone knows that Texas is a vast area of dry desert, rolling hills, pine-hardwood forests, coastal plains and grasslands. What everyone does not know is that Texas' natural areas are fast disappearing and, along with them, its wildlife, its elegant old trees — and its trails. This doesn't say much for those who have been responsible for the preservation of our natural resources, for those who were too preoccupied with oil and cattle (dollars and cents) to appraise and preserve Texas' most valuable asset. Many Texans have taken a startled look at what's left and are pleading for restoration and preservation of the natural ecosystems. Many Texans are having second thoughts about green plastic grass and concrete streambeds, and we hope with our book to convince you that there is nothing better than an honest-to-goodness tree and a muddy creekbottom with 'coon tracks and "crawdad" turrets.

This book is your key to hiking in almost all of the remaining natural areas. There are rigorous hikes from desert floor to mountain rim, easy hikes that loaf along creeks, hikes into hot canyons, up and down washes, through grasslands and to historic sites. Many of these hikes are relatively short, but keep in mind that it is not the distance you cover but what you see and remember that really counts.

All of these trails were hiked by us in 1974, and many of them were hiked in years past as well. Not all of the trails are clearly defined, making it necessary to stop and look for the route. Several of the hikes along the Lone Star Trail follow very obscure routes and could easily foil an inexperienced hiker. Also keep in mind that trails may become washed out or otherwise obliterated; civilization encroaches on others. Government agencies may, on occasion, modify parts of the routes.

HOW TO USE THIS BOOK

This book is intended to be merely an appetizer and a guide. Its purpose is to suggest possible hikes and outings. It is not a detailed description of each of the various trails and routes — such an endeavor would require a volume ten times the size of this. If you lose a trail or are not certain of a route, always (always) turn around and return to the trailhead rather than risk getting completely lost. The more you hike, the more expertise you'll develop in route finding.

All road mileages are approximate. We took these from our truck odometer, except in the case of Big Bend mileages which were provided by the National Park Service. Keep in mind that the odometers in various vehicles vary somewhat. If our description indicates that it is 9.0 miles to a trailhead, start keeping an eye out for it as you approach this mileage; but don't expect it to come up at exactly 9.0 miles. We measured all the trail mileages with a measuring wheel and are confident that they are more accurate than some of the trail signs.

Ease into hiking as you would any other sport. Begin with short outings and work your way gradually up to the longer treks. The times given for the various hikes are approximate;

slower hikers may need more time than indicated. There is no particular accomplishment in covering twenty miles in a day (we know some 10-year-olds who can do it with ease). The accomplishment lies in seeing and experiencing what's there and bringing back observations and memories that will last.

We have listed the "Elevation Change" for each hike as "Little," "Moderate" or "Considerable." These are somewhat arbitrary designations which don't correspond with exact altitudinal changes. Strong hikers might sneer at our "moderate" change; weak hikers might consider our "little" change to be understated.

If you have only a few spare hours, or if you are just passing through, take one of the shorter hikes, or sample the first part of one of the longer hikes. If you're suffering from an overdose of concrete and commercials, some of these hikes can provide you with a week's solitude.

DIFFERENT REGIONS

There is a tremendous variation from one area of Texas to another and from one altitude to the next. Although it is difficult to generalize, you will notice a number of distinct associations of plants and animals as you travel around the state, and if you want more than a nodding acquaintance, you'll find your pockets (like ours) are padded with more and more field guides. A pair of binoculars adds another, entirely different dimension to hiking.

Texas can be divided into several major areas in terms of topography and its associated flora and fauna. These are as follows:

TRANS-PECOS: The general area west of the Pecos River — the westernmost part of Texas. Included in the Trans-Pecos are Big Bend National Park, Guadalupe Mountains National Park and the Davis Mountains. The lower parts are Chihuahuan Desert from which you climb through grasslands, oak woodlands and pine forests.

PANHANDLE: The northernmost part of the state. Its grassy plains are cut here and there by canyons, such as Palo Duro.

EDWARDS PLATEAU: A large area in west-central Texas comprised of low, rolling limestone hills. Juniper is the dominant vegetation, but it is rapidly being gouged out of the landscape to increase forage to accommodate more cattle and sheep. Unless legislation can be passed to prevent wholesale clearing of the land, even on private property, the Edwards Plateau will become a dusty monument to the bulldozer.

SOUTH TEXAS: The general region south and east of the Edwards Plateau. Its vast stretches of mesquite and brushland attract several species of birds that can be seen nowhere else in the United States. Padre Island — the longest island for its width in the world — lies off the coast below Corpus Christi.

EAST TEXAS: Stretching from Aransas National Wildlife Refuge to the Louisiana border along the coast and inland west to about San Antonio and Fort Worth. Along the coast are the fast-disappearing lagoons and beaches and coastal prairies. Inland are pine forests (shortleaf, loblolly and longleaf) and deciduous forest (oaks, hickories, elms, beech, etc.). The animal life is more typical of the eastern United States than of the west. Here you'll encounter East Texas' nearsighted comic — the armadillo — and (in warm weather) ticks, chiggers, mosquitoes and water moccasins. Rainfall may average over 50 inches in this part of the state, compared to less than 10 inches for parts of the Trans-Pecos.

These regions (Trans-Pecos, Panhandle, Edwards Plateau, South Texas and East Texas) are only broad generalizations designed to give you a "handle" on hike planning.

LET'S SAVE A BIT OF TEXAS

You can drive for a hundred miles in some parts of Texas and see nothing but plowed ground. Cities and towns are expanding, most with no organization and with planning only as an afterthought. Lagoons, so vital to the entire ecology of the seas and to commercial fisheries, are fast succumbing to "Progress" — sacrificed to yacht clubs and condominiums at great expense to future generations.

The writing on the wall describes a barren and empty Texas in the 21st Century. Ranchers and farmers clear thousands of acres of mesquite and grassland and then add herbicides and pesticides to the environment. Yet, when concerned people want to set aside some of Texas' natural and wilderness areas, they face overwhelming opposition. If you are frightened by the spectre of Texas without trees, wildlife, lagoons (and people?), write your senators and congressmen and state officials.

Laws and enforcement preventing the removal of cacti from West Texas must be enacted soon. If not, the last specimens of a number of rare species will only be found on window sills of apartments in New York City. The bloke who dug them up will have a few extra dollars in his pocket, and the people who bought them will enjoy them until they are thrown out the next time they move. And we will all be the poorer for having lost some fascinating components of the desert — components which have taken ten thousand years to develop their present form.

Logging is an undeniable necessity in the world as we know it. Even to preserve the industry, wise management must be employed. As we hiked (and hiked and hiked) through East Texas, it was apparent that there was much more damage to the environment as a result of hauling the cut timber out than from the removal of the trees themselves. Texas' forests are a maze of log roads which are also open invitations to four-wheel drive vehicles and motorcycles. Ballooning is expensive, but that or a similar method should be required for logging.

SEASONS AND WATER

Most of the hikes described in this book would be most enjoyable if made in the fall, winter or spring. Texas is very hot in the summer. We do not generally recommend summer hiking for others, but we confess to doing it quite regularly ourselves. Consider short, early-morning hikes in the summer; do not consider backpacks in hot areas. If in doubt about conditions, a call to the appropriate local government agency may be of some help.

Anytime from March onward you can expect daytime temperatures to exceed 100 degrees in the Trans-Pecos. Lots of drinking water is needed at this time. On all hikes, we suggest that you carry all the water needed for the entire trip and not depend on springs and streams. On a two-mile outing, a gallon of water might seem like a lot until you sprain an ankle and need six hours in the sun to get back. Then that water could save your life. Learn the symptoms of heat exhaustion and heat stroke; also, learn how to prevent them.

BIG BEND AND GUADALUPE MOUNTAINS NATIONAL PARKS

These two great natural areas are administered by the National Park Service, an agency for which we have great admiration. It is unfortunate that other governmental agencies cannot attract individuals of the calibre that are drawn to the Park Service. We suggest that you check with a ranger before going on any lengthy hikes in these areas. Overnight camping permits are required in both, and there is (or soon will be) a limitation on overnight backcountry usage. We support this policy wholeheartedly, even if it means that we, too, must wait our turn. Use only gas stoves for cooking; do not use open campfires. All plants and animals, all geological and archaeological features are completely protected. Big Bend and the Guadalupes are some of nature's last bastions in Texas, and your respect will bring rewards that are greater than anything money can buy. Hikes 1-14 are in Big Bend; Hikes 19-20 are in the Guadalupes.

MAPS

The maps are drawn from a variety of sources and are intended to be general guides only. Most are not drawn to scale. Routes are indicated by dashed lines, and North is indicated by a directional arrow.

Topographic maps are available for Big Bend and Guadalupe Mountains National Parks. The U.S. Forest Service and Texas Parks and Wildlife Department provide maps for many of their areas, and interpretive sheets and guides are often available for the asking or at the trailheads.

ACKNOWLEDGEMENTS

We want to thank most of all the individuals and organizations who have fought to preserve some of natural Texas. We also want to thank those who are carrying on against all the odds (mainly the almighty dollar and personal gain) and those who are using foresight in planning more wisely for the future.

In particular, we wish to extend our appreciation to Emil Kindschy, Paul Conn and Brom Wilkins and their team of 14 section leaders for the information furnished on the Lone Star Trail; also to Jane Kittleman for information on Lake Texoma and to Rick Lobello and Dale Evans for pictures on Apache Canyon and the East Texas trails.

THERE'S A LOT TO ENJOY

And we hope *50 HIKES IN TEXAS* helps you to enjoy it.

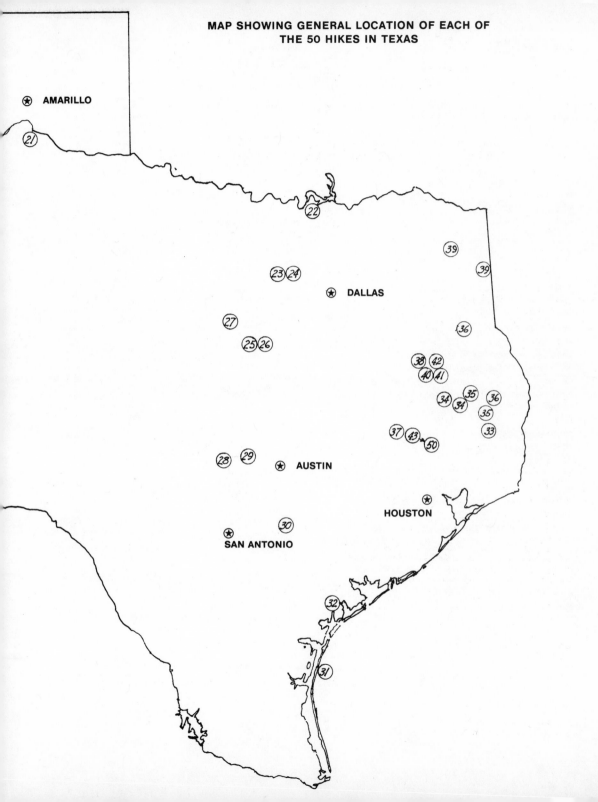

MAP SHOWING GENERAL LOCATION OF EACH OF
THE 50 HIKES IN TEXAS

DAY HIKES

It is possible (but not practical) to take off for an entire day with no special equipment at all. Because we are comfort-loving and because emergencies do occur, we take the following items with us on all outings, no matter how short. This is not intended to be a comprehensive list; you can add or delete items to tailor it to your own needs.

1) Begin with a good quality, comfortable daypack of lightweight material which is large enough to corral all your gear. 2) Canteens come in different sizes and shapes, but the most important thing to consider is that one gallon of water per day per person is considered a minimum during hot weather. 3) Salty foods or salt tablets may be helpful during hot weather, but be sure to check with your physician first. 4) Snakebite is relatively rare, but a good kit with knowledge of treatments is a wise idea in Texas. 5) To a complete first aid kit, add a knee brace or elastic bandage. 6) Emergency food. 7) Wear comfortable, broken-in footwear. Be sure that footwear is warm enough for cold weather and that the soles have a good tread. High boots might deflect a snake, but they are no guarantee of safety. 8) A hat and long-sleeved shirt offer some protection from the sun in summer. 9) Long pants of a tough material help to prevent scratches, scrapes and insect bites. 10) Sunglasses. 11) Down jacket, gloves and long underwear are on the winter list. 12) Flashlight with extra batteries and bulb. 13) Matches in a waterproof container. 14) This guide (of course), maps, plant and animal field guides. 15) Camera and accessories. 16) Binoculars. 17) Toilet items. 18) Insect repellent. 19) A plastic litter bag with drawstring closure should be tied to the outside of your pack for easy access. Haul out everything you take in — and a little more, please.

Daypack, canteens and litter bag

BACKPACKS

Once, when the country was new, it was an art to live off the land. Hikers of a century ago could take off into the wilderness for weeks with not much more than a simple bedroll and a few provisions. Now the land is fragmented, with only tidbits of wilderness left; and today's hikers must practice a new art — self-sufficiency. Trees can no longer be cut down to provide a night's shelter, but it is fortunate that they no longer need to be. Plants and animals can no longer provide meals, nor do they have to. Downed wood cannot be spared for campfires, but self-contained hikers don't need wood.

Outdoor stores are popping up like mushrooms, and they offer a sophisticated assortment of down clothing, sleeping bags, super tents, fancy stoves and intricate gadgets. This presents a problem — what to buy and what not to buy. And when you've surmounted that, there's a new problem — what to take and what to leave home. From the loads we've seen some hikers carry, they appear to have brought along everything, just in case. Keep in mind that enjoyment is the object of hiking, and you don't want to be irritated and pre-occupied by too heavy a load. Experience is the best teacher when it comes to provisioning yourself for different climates and terrains.

The most important factor in the selection of a 1) backpack should be comfort. Size is another thing to consider, but it should make no difference whether the pack is olive drab or red, white and blue. Be suspicious of a cheap bag. A lightweight, fine quality 2) tent contributes a lot to comfort; but you should definitely equip it with a 3) rainfly to insure its usefulness. Selection of a 4) sleeping bag depends on the weather. There are occasions during summer when no bag whatsoever is needed. For cold weather, our choice is always a goose down bag because it has the highest insulating quality for its weight. Some people sleep "warm," and some people sleep "cold." You will have to experiment to see what type of bag is best for you under different conditions. Many areas prohibit the use of firewood because it plays several important roles in the natural scheme of things. All back-country campfires should be (and probably will be) prohibited. A small 5) stove is the answer. There are several excellent ones that weigh very little and are much more efficient than a campfire for cooking. A 6) fuel container especially designed for fuel should be used with the stove. Be sure that it is labeled. You may want to consider taking salami, jerky, cheese and other foods that don't need to be cooked. Leave all canned foods where they belong — at home. A good 7) ground mat is imperative in cold weather, otherwise every part of your body which contacts the ground will be cold. Avoid air mattresses and all their problems of inflation, leaks, etc. Be sure to bring 8) all items that you would take for a day hike with the exception of the daypack itself. Don't forget to consider 9) overnight camping permits, campfire permits and a 10) litter bag tied to the outside of your pack for easy access. When you leave your campsite there should be no evidence of your having been there.

A typical backpack campsite

AGENCIES AND ORGANIZATIONS

Aransas National Wildlife Refuge
P.O. Box 68
Austwell, Texas 77950

The Superintendent
Big Bend National Park
Texas 79834

Caddo Lake State Park
Box 316
Karnack, Texas 75661

Denison Resident Office
Corps of Engineers
Drawer A
Denison, Texas 75020

Daingerfield State Park
P.O. Box B
Daingerfield, Texas 75638

Davis Mountains State Park
Box 786
Fort Davis, Texas 79734

Davy Crockett National Forest
Neches District
East Loop 304
Crockett, Texas 75835

Dinosaur Valley State Park
Box 396
Glen Rose, Texas 76043

Fort Davis National Historic Site
Fort Davis, Texas 79734

Fort Worth Nature Center & Refuge
Route 10, Box 53
Fort Worth, Texas 76135

Guadalupe Mountains National Park
c/o Superintendent
Carlsbad Caverns National Park
P.O. Box 1598
Carlsbad, New Mexico 88220

Huntsville State Park
P.O. Box 508
Huntsville, Texas 77340

LBJ State Park
Box 201
Stonewall, Texas 78671

Meridian State Park
P.O. Box 188
Meridian, Texas 76665

Mission Tejas State Park
Route 2, Box 108
Grapeland, Texas 75844

Monahans Sandhills State Park
Box 1738
Monahans, Texas 79756

Padre Island National Seashore
10235 South Padre Island Drive
Corpus Christi, Texas 78418

Palmetto State Park
P.O. Box 4
Ottine, Texas 78658

Palo Duro State Park
Route 2, Box 114
Canyon, Texas 79015

Pedernales Falls State Park
Route 1, Box 31-A
Johnson City, Texas 78636

Sam Houston National Forest
Big Thicket District
P.O. Box 817 (Farm Road 2025)
Cleveland, Texas 77327

Sam Houston National Forest
Raven District
P.O. Box 393 (Farm Road 1375)
New Waverly, Texas 77358

Texas Forestry Association
P.O. Box 1488
Lufkin, Texas 75901

Texas Parks & Wildlife Department
John H. Reagan Building
Austin, Texas 78701

BOOKS FOR ADDITIONAL READING

A knowledge of the flora and fauna can greatly enhance any hike. We have found the following publications to be especially interesting and helpful:

Burt, William Henry and Richard P. Grossenheider. 1964. *A Field Guide to the Mammals.* Houghton Mifflin, Boston.

Conant, Roger. 1958. *A Field Guide to the Reptiles and Amphibians of Eastern North America.* Houghton Mifflin, Boston.

Douglas, William O. 1967. *Farewell to Texas: A Vanishing Wilderness.* McGraw-Hill, New York.

Irwin, Howard S. 1961. *Roadside Flowers of Texas.* University of Texas Press, Austin.

Little (Jr.), Elbert L. 1950. *Southwestern Trees: A Guide to the Native Species of New Mexico and Arizona.* U.S. Dept. of Agriculture.

Murie, Olaus J. 1954. *A Field Guide to Animal Tracks.* Houghton Mifflin, Boston.

Peterson, Roger Tory. 1963. *A Field Guide to the Birds of Texas.* Houghton Mifflin, Boston.

Peterson, Roger Tory and James Fisher. 1956. *Wild America.* Houghton Mifflin, Boston.

Robbins, Chandler S., Bertel Bruun and Herbert S. Zim. 1966. *Birds of North America.* Golden Press, New York.

Stebbins, Robert C. 1966. *A Field Guide to Western Reptiles and Amphibians.* Houghton Mifflin, Boston.

Texas Forest Service. 1971. *Forest Trees of Texas: How to Know Them.* College Station.

Warnock, Barton H. and Peter Koch. 1970. *Wildflowers of the Big Bend Country, Texas.* Sul Ross State University, Alpine.

Wauer, Roland H. 1973. *Birds of Big Bend National Park and Vicinity.* University of Texas Press, Austin.

Wauer, Roland H. 1973. *Naturalist's Big Bend.* Peregrine Productions, Santa Fe.

Werler, John E. 1964. *Poisonous Snakes of Texas and First Aid Treatment of their Bites.* Texas Parks & Wildlife Department, Austin.

1 SOUTH RIM

Distance — 12.0 Miles Round Trip
Time — 11 Hours
Elevation Change — Considerable

The southwestern edge of the Chisos Mountains is a precipitous drop of 2,500 feet to the desert floor. It offers a spectacular view of Big Bend country and of Mexico beyond. The South Rim Trail is a long hike and involves a hefty gain in elevation — not suitable for the casual hiker but very rewarding for the determined hiker in excellent condition.

To reach the Basin trailhead, proceed west from park headquarters 3.4 miles, and turn left on the road to the Basin which is another 6.5 miles. The trailhead is near the ranger station and is signed.

Take the left fork. When you have come 0.2 mile, take the right fork toward Laguna Meadow. The route climbs gradually at first, then more and more steeply as it works to gain the saddle at 3 miles. Just beyond the saddle, at 3.5 miles, is Laguna Meadow which is a good place to rest and look around before continuing on.

The trail is still uphill as it moves out of the meadow, beyond an old mescal pit on the left, to a junction with the Blue Creek Trail at 3.7 miles, and to a junction with a side trail which short-cuts over to Boot Springs at 4.3 miles. Keep right here, and continue another 1.7 miles out to the South Rim, which is signed. From this point you have a sweeping view which takes in Santa Elena Canyon some 20 miles away to the west; Emory Peak to the north; and the Sierra del Carmen, in Mexico, to the east. The dark range behind the Sierra del Carmen is the Fronterizas. Dodson Ranch is a small speck in the desert below you; and on a clear day, you can see peaks 75 miles away in Mexico.

When you reach the East Rim junction, stay left toward Boot Springs, and soon the trail begins a gradual drop into the canyon. This is a fragile area of intense interest to biologists. Birdwatchers come from all over the country to see the Colima Warbler. The route passes a catchment dam left over from ranching days, the Juniper Canyon Trail junction (keep left), and the fire patrol cabin at Boot Springs (7.7 miles).

There is a gradual climb from Boot Springs to a pass 1.2 miles beyond. Enroute, you pass the "boot" and hike through some of the prettiest country in the park — big boulders banked with brown leaves, winding path, shady bends. From the pass, the trail plummets directly down to the Basin 3.2 miles beyond. The descent is steep at first, then tapers off as you pass Boulder Meadow (keep left), cross Juniper Flat, and pass the Chisos Loop Trail junction (keep right). At 11.7 miles, you join the loop with the trail you took earlier, turn right and complete the short distance back to the trailhead.

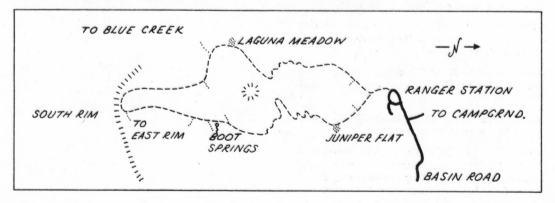

View from South Rim

2   APACHE CANYON

Distance — 9 Miles Round Trip
Time — 10 Hours
Elevation Change — Moderate
Topographic Maps — The Basin, Texas
                            Tule Mountain, Texas

Apache Canyon is a small but colorful canyon emptying to the north from the western portion of Burro Mesa. The trail to Apache Canyon follows the old Burro Mesa Road (no longer open to vehicles). It climbs onto the mesa near its extreme eastern point and crosses to the west before curving north to end near Apache Canyon.

The trail head is reached by driving 4.9 miles south from Santa Elena Junction toward Castolon. The trail starts at a metal fence post-marker on the west side of the road, across from the road-side parking area. From the trail head the old road can be seen climbing steeply the 150 feet or so onto the mesa.

Burro Mesa is named for the wild burros that grazed there in times past. The mesa is a block of the earth's surface which has sunk, relative to the surrounding terrain, due to faulting. The road along the east side of the mesa follows part of the fault line. The lava which caps the higher points on Burro Mesa is part of the same lava deposit which caps Emory Peak, highest point in the park. Its elevation on Emory peak is about 3500 feet above this same formation on Burro Mesa.

Once past the short, steep climb onto the mesa, trail gradients are gentle, when compared to many hiking trails in Big Bend. Burro Mesa is not flat on top, so the trail has many ups and downs, crossing alternate low ridges and drainages.

Much of the vegetation along the trail is the familiar lechuguilla, creosote bush, white thorned acacia, sotol, and short grasses. These xerophytic plants are surprisingly beautiful in spite of their hardiness.

About 4 miles from the starting point the trail drops into a broad, flat, high valley. The center portion of this valley is green with a mesquite and creosote bush thicket. Before reaching the dense vegetation, you will see to your right some willow and cottonwood trees that are growing in and around a dry stock tank (pond). The inside of the tank offers a good winter campsite, with grassy carpet and shelter from the cold wind, within the tree-lined banks. (In some months, particularly September, biting flies can be a plague on the mesa in and around the stock tank.)

Only portions of the road can be found after it enters the thicket. It will be easier to follow foot paths or pick your own route the half-mile or so to Apache Canyon.

There is a large corral with a stone wall at least 3 feet thick to the left of the trail shortly after it enters the thicket. It is definitely worth the short detour to see this structure. As the trail emerges from the north side of the thicket, there is, to the west on a slight rise near the corner of a low mesa, what remains of a stone ranch house.

Water can sometimes be found in tinajas toward the western end of the drainage which is just south of the ranch house.

Apache Canyon begins north of the end of the low mesa behind the ranch house, which is west of the road (trail). Portions of the canyon are brilliantly colored, with tints ranging from yellow and orange, to purple. Apache Canyon is spectacular when viewed from within the canyon itself or from the rim. The canyon can be entered with little difficulty near its upper end.

A possible alternate hike out of Apache Canyon and off Burro Mesa, rather than retracing the route in, would be to walk 5 miles north from the bottom end of the canyon to the paved road (if you have stationed a car there ahead of time).

As you walk near the canyon you will find areas where the ground is literally covered with flint. The numerous flint chips indicate that this area was an important source of material for tools and weapons, used by the indians who once inhabited this area. Remember, the flint, like all rocks and artifacts in the park, is protected and should be left in place.

This is a suggestion that may appeal to some hikers: The trail onto Burro Mesa is so distinct that is can be easily followed by moonlight (don't use a flashlight — learn to walk in the moonlight without one). A night-time hike provides the possibility of going onto or off of Burro Mesa in hot weather, when the moon is "right".

Apache Canyon

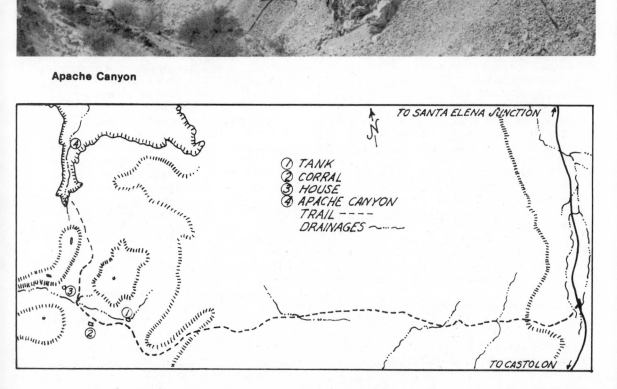

TO SANTA ELENA JUNCTION

N

① TANK
② CORRAL
③ HOUSE
④ APACHE CANYON
TRAIL - - - -
DRAINAGES ·—·—·

TO CASTOLON

3 THE WINDOW ✓

Distance — 5.5 Miles Round Trip
Time — 4 Hours
Elevation Change — Moderate

The Chisos Basin is a depression surrounded on all sides by mountains and ridges. All of the rainfall (average 15.7 inches per year) that runs off these high places collects in Oak Creek and shoots out a narrow notch in the lower end of the Basin — "The Window." An occasional winter storm may leave from a few inches to a record 20 inches of snow in the area, and this runoff also exits through The Window.

From the trailhead in the Basin (see Hike 1), hike downhill to the right. Various grasses, snakeweed, whitebrush, a few junipers and pinyons and Engelmann's pricklypears grow along the trail. After a short distance, the trail switchbacks down to the rear of the stables; and there is a little canyon on the left that seems to appeal to several different species of birds. You have come about 0.4 mile at this point.

Continuing down past the campground, you swing near the sewage lagoon which is attractive to ravens and turkey vultures. At this point, about 1.0 mile from the start of the hike, a trail from the campground comes in from the right. If you thought all the cactus wrens were

beaking into things at the campground, you were wrong — a number of the comical critters are deployed along the trail to heckle hikers and to keep a beady eye on the boots and saddle set.

The grade, while gradual, is decidedly downhill all the way. The trail gets heavy use from the horses so that you have to watch your step and contend with powdery dust. When you have come 1.7 miles, the trail moves into the welcome shade of trees in the canyon bottom and, about 0.2 mile further, drops into the sandy bottom of Oak Creek with its large permanent fixtures of rock and oak.

Near the 2.2-mile mark, there is a tallus slope of red rock which is in marked contrast to neighboring cliffs. As you close the distance to The Window, the craggy rock walls of the canyon begin to close down on the trail. The horses are parked at the 2.6-mile mark where they run out of suitable footing.

Now you start into the polished-rock mouth of the chute where little pools of water collect in rock retainers and rock steps have been made to guarantee safe footing. (Don't drink the water.) The canyon walls form a slot about 20 feet wide at The Window. Stay back of the warning sign which is there for a good reason — the slippery rock and a sheer drop.

If you return to the Basin in late afternoon, you can watch the sunset through The Window.

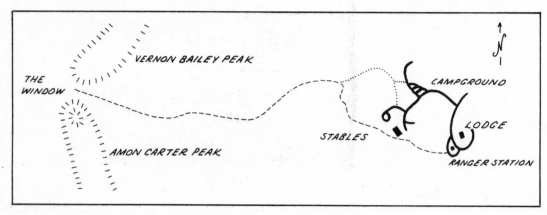

The Window

4   LOST MINE

Distance — 4.7 Miles Round Trip
Time — 5 Hours
Elevation Change — Considerable

Many southwestern hikes have a legendary focal point — buried strongboxes, stolen payrolls and lost mines. The legends add to the atmosphere of the hikes but, to our knowledge, have not added to anyone's recent wealth or fame. The Lost Mine Trail climbs (rather steeply in places) to a rocky viewpoint from which you can see Lost Mine Peak in particular and a large part of Big Bend in general. The interpretive booklet at the trailhead makes this hike a good introduction to the Chisos.

From headquarters in Big Bend, drive west on the main park road for 3.4 miles to Basin Road. Proceed 5.0 miles up Basin Road to parking for Lost Mine Trail on the left. The route is easy to follow. You won't need any help from us to get from the bottom to the top and back again, so we thought this would be a good place to tell you about some of the special things to watch for that make hiking more than just good exercise.

When you hike day after day for a living, you would soon come to hate it if you didn't learn to look for and appreciate a number of small things — a cactus in bloom, an oriole swinging on a yucca or a storm building in the distance. When you have hiked 40 miles and the week's not over, you don't just step over a velvet ant

on the trail — you hunker down and inspect her from stem to stern (without touching; she is actually a wasp and can inflict a painful sting).

With extraordinary good luck, you could see a mountain lion in the early morning or evening. The lithe cats have been hunted to the brink of extinction, but rare sightings have occurred near the beginning of this hike.

We are not birdwatchers in the true sense, but birds are one of the most frequent diversions on our hikes. When we reached the saddle at the 0.8-mile mark, we spotted a sparrow hawk riding the updrafts in Juniper Canyon. To the casual observer, the sparrow hawk is just a little brown-and-white hawk. But in the binoculars he is a beautifully-marked little falcon with large, dark eyes. He's a colorful bird with touches of black, rusty orange and steely blue. He came to hover directly above, almost perfectly still on the air, and it was obvious that he was inspecting us as we were him.

Later, when we reached the end of the trail (about 2.4 miles), there he was again, coasting on the currents below us. As we ate lunch, he flew in to perch on a rock outcropping nearby. We were pleased with him, not because he was a bird to add to a list but because we were able to watch him going about his business and because he was obviously watching us go about ours. These are the small experiences that add up over the years to many good hours of remembering.

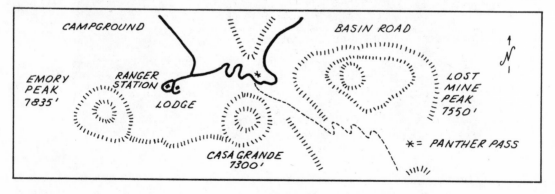

End of Lost Mine Trail

5   JUNIPER CANYON

Distance — 11.8 Miles Round Trip
Time — 10 Hours
Elevation Change — Considerable

Juniper Canyon Trail is a desert-to-rim hike which connects with the South Rim Trail in the Chisos Mountains. It is a very steep hike with almost no switchbacks to soften the grade; and we don't recommend it to any but the most experienced and durable hikers. For those, it is a fine hike through some very pretty country.

From park headquarters, take the main road east 5.3 miles, and turn right on Glenn Springs Road. You're on dirt roads from here on in, and they are pretty rough in spots. Proceed 7.1 miles to a sign which says "Juniper Canyon." Turn right here and continue for 6 miles to parking and a sign which indicates Dodson Trail to the left (see Hike 6) and Juniper Canyon Trail straight ahead. The first part of the trail is still a two-track road. Hopefully, it will be closed to vehicular traffic and one track allowed to overgrow so that only a foot trail remains.

The actual trailhead is a far piece (3 miles) from the trail proper which ascends Juniper Canyon. As you hike along the road, you gradually gain altitude. The spiky lechuguillas, agaves and sotol begin to mingle with the softer mesquites, junipers and pinyons.

When you have come 3 miles, the road ends,

and a footpath takes off on the right. It is a no-nonsense hike from here to the top. As you climb the brushy side of the canyon, you pass Upper Juniper Spring where old relics from ranching days rot in the shade of big oaks. Mexican jays and band-tailed pigeons share the canyon with numerous other birds and animals. There are several spots where jumbles of big boulders and deep leaves in the creek bottom invite you to rest your bones and savor the scenery.

About 3.8 miles from the start, the trail crosses the usually-dry creek near a dead juniper snag and continues the very steep climb up the side of the Chisos. Clumpy grass, mountain mahogany and sumac offer little shade on this part of the hike.

At about the 5-mile mark, little rolly rocks on the trail require some fancy footwork. The stinkbug approach, which employs hands as well as feet, works quite well. Half a mile beyond here, you finally crest the saddle and continue for a way on relatively flat ground. Soon the route drops down and joins the South Rim Trail about 600 feet from Boot Springs (to the right). Do not depend on Boot Springs for water as there usually is none.

The return hike is via the same route, although it is possible to go from Boot Springs to the Chisos Basin (see Hike 1). To do this, it would be necessary to have made transportation arrangements in advance.

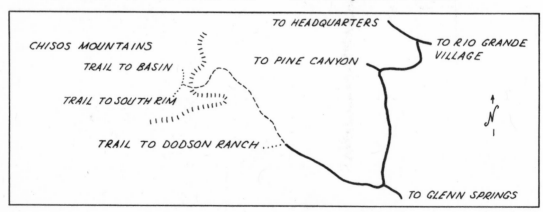

Havard Agave

6   DODSON RANCH

Distance — 7.8 Miles Round Trip
Time — 7 Hours
Change in Elevation — Moderate

Big Bend was cattle country in the past. The Estado Land and Cattle Company had cattle here in 1885, and by the 1920's there were many other ranches on the grasslands around the Chisos Mountains. Eventually the area became less desirable, largely as a result of overgrazing. Grazing was last permitted in 1945, but about 20,000 cattle and an almost equal number of goats as well as several thousand sheep were in the area then. The land was so severely overgrazed that portions of it still have not recovered today.

The Dodson place is the site of one such ranch that was in operation from around 1919 to 1943. Little remains today other than parts of several tumble-down houses, an old corral and scattered fence posts.

To reach the trailhead, follow directions to the Juniper Canyon parking area (see Hike 5). Dodson Ranch Trail is the left fork here. The first 800 feet are on an old two-track road, but from there it is a trail. Vegetation along the route includes various grasses, lechuguilla, sotol, candelilla, yucca, pricklypear, several species of hedgehogs, Mormon tea, agave, ocotillo and mesquite. Canyon wrens have staked their claims to many of the washes along the route. They aren't bashful about challenging hikers with reedy calls and a great deal of bouncing around the rocks.

The general trend is slightly up. You drop in and out of a number of washes and trend over and alongside low hills. In many places the route follows up drainages. In some places it is easy to lose the trail, and a careful search for rock cairns is required.

At a bit over 3.3 miles, the route comes to a little saddle and drops into a wash on the other side. There are several confusing trails of use here. Go right, up the wash, for about 200 feet; turn left, out of the wash, and follow the trail over the next ridge as it curves to the right into the next drainage. You can then see the old corral and crumbling buildings in a small copse of trees in the canyon on the left. The trail drops into the wash and up to the buildings.

As you'll discover on the hike in, this is about the only shade around, and it's a haven for birds and other animals as well as for hikers. There is a small spring next to a drooping juniper not far from the house, but it's not reliable. Please leave no sign of your having been there, and return by the same route.

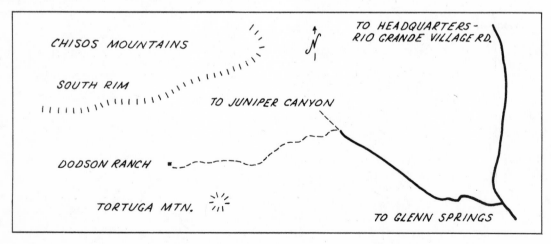

Dodson Ranch

MARCH 1978
WITH MIKE & MARY HILGER,
JIM DAWES, C'LEE.

Distance — 1.4 Miles Round Trip
Time — 1 Hour
Elevation Change — Little

Boquillas Canyon is a creation of the Rio Grande — 25 miles long, 1,200 feet deep, and elegant. The hike into the canyon is very short, but any hike in the southwest that has water as its destination is worth checking out. And the canyon is situated near the Sierra del Carmen mountains which, when combined with the evening sun, explode into geological fireworks of rose and gold.

From park headquarters, drive south 19.1 miles. Turn left on a road signed "Boquillas Canyon," and continue 3.8 miles to parking. (Keep left at the fork where another road goes right to Boquillas Crossing. The Crossing goes to the little Mexican town of Boquillas on the far side of the river.)

The trailhead is signed where it takes off from the parking lot. It climbs for about 0.1 mile, then rounds the flank of the hill and descends to the river. At the foot of the hill, just before you head toward the canyon, look closely at the rocks on the right. There are several round holes in them where the Indians

have ground corn.

Reeds, willows, mesquites and tamarisks grow in dense thickets along the trail, killdeers run up and down the sand bars and cry plaintively, and the trail is a path of fine sand. Because of the sand, the route may be a little obscure in places, but the object is just to follow the river into the mouth of the canyon.

The large animal that watches your progress from the thickets is the Mexican horse. He is a great believer in the old "grass-is-greener" philosophy and is continually ranging from one side of the river to the other.

When you have come 0.5 mile, the trail enters the mouth of the canyon and follows a pebbled beach. To your left, at the base of the sheer canyon wall, is a big sand dune — offspring of wind and the sandy flood plain. There is a little hollow in the canyon wall at the top of the dune.

The trail continues through more flood plain vegetation, skirts the base of the cliff, and comes to an abrupt halt where the cliff meets the river. From here, you can return to the parking lot by the same route — or dally by the river, or climb the dune, or just loll in the shade and contemplate such things as the philosophy of the Mexican horse.

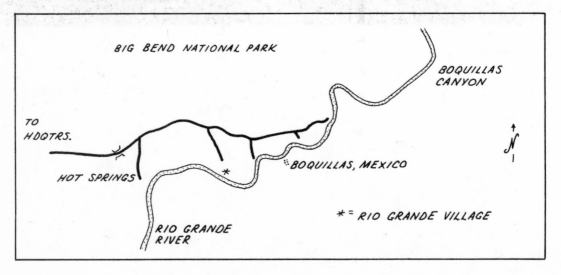

Boquillas Canyon

8   MULE EARS SPRING

Distance — 3.8 Miles Round Trip
Time — 4 Hours
Elevation Change — Moderate
Topographic Map — Cerro Castellan

Without the water provided by the scattered springs and tinajas, the Big Bend country would have been uninhabitable (away from the river). And, because they provided this necessity of life in such arid land, most of the dependable springs became the sites for isolated ranch houses and corrals. Often the water from the larger springs was also piped to other parts of a ranch for livestock — and man. Mule Ears Spring is such a place.

There are the remains of a ranch house immediately above the spring, and on the west side of the drainage is what remains of a stone corral. The section of trail approaching Mule Ears Spring follows the route of a pipeline that carried water to a stock tank located some distance downstream. These "improvements" were made when the spring and surrounding country were a part of the Castolon Ranch.

Water which falls on the adjacent terrain percolates down through the porous soil until it reaches an impervious layer of volcanic ash, on top of which it flows laterally to emerge as the spring.

The spring gets its name from two nearby peaks which were formed when two volcanic dikes and surrounding area were eroded, leaving pinacles. These "ears", which were composed of harder rock, were left standing. The name, Mule Ears Peaks, is fitting for their configuration.

This is a desert hike, with no shade between car and spring, and is not recommended for hot weather. In the summer, early morning temperatures are usually cool and hiking then is a real pleasure. But, later in the day it can become unbearably hot, making the distance from Mule Ears Spring to the car a most unpleasant and potentially hazardous trip.

The trail starts at Mule Ears overlook parking area, which is just off the paved road to Castolon. The trail skirts around the south side of Trap Mountain and crosses a number of dry washes along the foot of the slope. Part of the trail follows the route of an old road which led to the old ranch near the spring.

At approximately 0.9 miles from the start is a trail junction with a less prominent trail taking off to the right (south). Keep left, and remember this junction on your return. At about 1.1 miles from the start the trail drops into the drainage from Trap Spring and Mule Ears Spring and follows it for a short distance. After emerging from this arroyo onto higher ground, the green vegetation, primarily mesquite, surrounding Trap Spring can be seen a short distance to the left (north) of the trail. A side trip to this spring is short (no trail) and rewarding. For the next half-mile the trail is relatively flat, gaining elevation gradually. It drops back into the drainage, which it follows for a short distance, climbing up the north bank near the stone corral, and Mule Ears Spring.

The trail crosses the drainage just below the spring, but is not so heavily used beyond this point. There is water and shade at the spring. The green mesquite, willow trees, Bermuda grass, and many other plants make this an extremely beautiful oasis in the desert. When the flowering trees and plants are in bloom the buzzing of bees is continuous. Colorful animals to be seen include the collared lizard and the varied bunting (usually singing around the spring, even in the heat of the day). Please be gentle with the plants and animals of the spring, and disturb them as little as possible during your visit.

Mule Ears Peaks

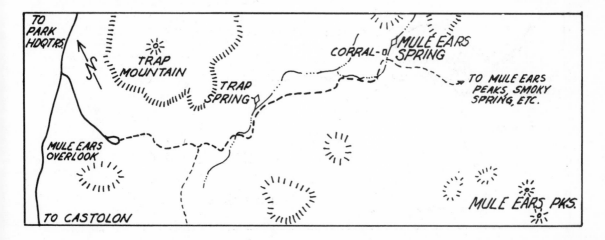

Distance — 3.1 Miles Round Trip
Time — 3 Hours
Elevation Change — Very Little

This wash drains much of the eastern part of Big Bend National Park. It would be possible to hike from Upper Tornillo Creek where it crosses the park road to Lower Tornillo Creek Bridge. This is a distance of some 24 miles. The shorter hike described here will give you a good introduction to the area.

From park headquarters in Big Bend, drive east 16.1 miles to Lower Tornillo Creek Bridge. Park on either side of the bridge. The wash is usually dry, but it is no place to be during a summer cloudburst. Tornillo can turn into a raging river with water lapping at the upper portions of the bridge.

There is no exact route here. Simply hike downstream along the wash, and wander back and forth to check out various things which draw your attention. The bed of the wash consists of sand, scoured stones, debris left in the wake of summer floods, and mud that has dried and cracked. Texas' appraiser, the turkey vulture, will probably look you over from above. Mesquite, catclaw acacia, Guayacan, desert-willow and seepwillow crowd along the banks. In many places where the banks have eroded you can get a good view of the root systems of many species of trees. Some of these systems are much longer and more extensive below ground than above.

Just beyond 1.0 mile, the creek turns left, and its right bank is a tall limestone-shale cliff. The softer shale has eroded more deeply, accenting the thin, flat layers of limestone. In some spots the rock is encrusted with pretty but crumbly calcite crystals.

A number of springs between here and the Rio Grande create little pools in an otherwise dry wash. In contrast to the dry creek bed which is frosted with alkalai, the pools teem with green algae and darting minnows. Ducks like this spot, and cliff swallows nest in the cliff overhangs. Leopard frogs plunk into the water as you pass.

The wash empties into the Rio Grande near the historic Hot Springs complex.

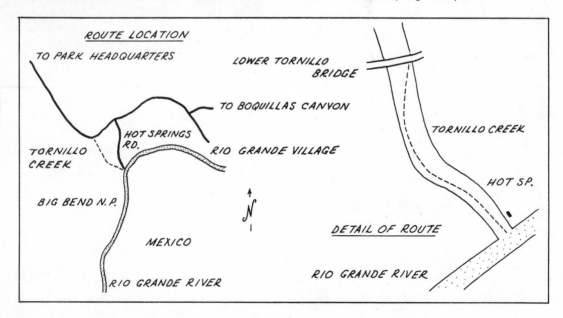

Lower Tornillo Wash

Distance — 1.0 Mile Round Trip
Time — 2 Hours
Elevation Change — Little

A pouroff is simply that — a narrow chute where a wash empties over a cliff after a storm. In Big Bend where water is in short supply, the pouroff is usually just a dry chimney of polished rock; but after a heavy storm, it becomes a howling drop for the mesa runoff. This pouroff is at the head of a box canyon.

From park headquarters, drive west 13.2 miles to Castolon Road. Head south 11.4 miles to Burro Mesa Pouroff Road on the right. The trailhead is 1.8 miles in at the end of this road.

The trail heads out over flat creosotebush desert toward a ragged cut in the mesa ahead. Layered cliffs move in on the right, and the desert floor is studded with large rocks that have fallen from above. Ocotillos, chollas and pricklypears mingle with the creosotebush, and the short grass with tufts is fluffgrass. No hike in Big Bend during hot weather is complete without a turkey vulture or two eyeing you from above.

Look for candelilla beside the trail on the right as you start across a wash. It resembles a clump of thin, gray-green tapers. Mesquite and desert hackberry eke out an existence along here.

Just a little over a quarter mile from the start, turn right and go up the sandy wash where traces of trail may or may not be apparent. The wash rarely runs, but the occasional water is enough to nurture mountain buckeye (poisonous fruit), acacia and desertwillow. Burro Mesa looms high on your left.

A quarter mile up the wash, you are treated to a spectacular view of the pouroff as your eyes travel up the long shaft of polished rock to the mesa top. The softer rock at the base where you are standing has eroded to widen the drop at the bottom, but the erosion-resistant rhyolite rock higher up maintains the narrow, half-cylinder shape of the pouroff. This is really an interesting-ominous spot, especially if it's a cloudy day and you have a good imagination.

On the return, you can see a big gash in the distant mesa to your right and ahead as you approach the parking lot. This is Santa Elena Canyon (see Hike 14).

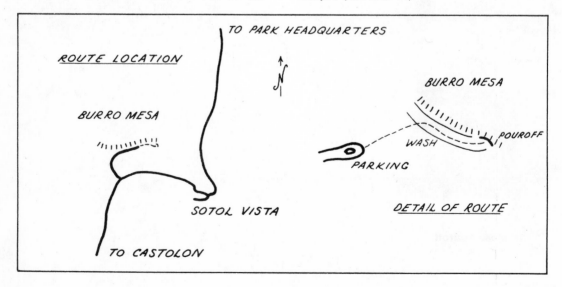

Burro Mesa Pouroff

11 BURRO SPRINGS

Distance — 2.3 Miles Round Trip
Time — 2 Hours
Elevation Change — Little

Many species of wildlife in the desert depend on springs for water — and springs are few and far between in Big Bend. This hike takes you through a mile of bone dry desert to a point which overlooks the green evidence of springs.

From park headquarters, drive west 13.2 miles to Castolon Road. Head south 11.4 miles to Burro Mesa Pouroff Road on the right, and proceed 1.1 miles to Burro Springs parking on the left.

The trail is easy to follow as it moves out across the creosotebush desert. Big Bend's usual desert plants are here: lechuguilla, Engelmann's and purple pricklypear, Torrey yucca, cholla, ocotillo, fluffgrass and Texas ranger. As you cross a little wash near the outset of the hike, compare the meager growth of desertwillows and catclaws here with the cottonwoods and seepwillows that grow in the same wash at the hike's end. Spindly Christmas chollas grow beside the trail on the right as it leaves the wash.

The trail climbs a little as it maneuvers around the base of a hill. The hillside is covered with dark volcanic rock and clumpy chino grass. When you have come 0.7 mile from the trailhead, you are behind the hill, and the trail drops into a little canyon. Still trending left, you skirt the base of some 100-foot cliffs of craggy black rock on the left and a wash to the right.

The trail ends high above a narrow canyon where fair-sized trees grow in the sandy stream bed. If you time your hike so that you're perched here at dawn or dusk, you should be able to see some of the animals that come here for water — javelinas, coyotes, gray foxes and mule deer.

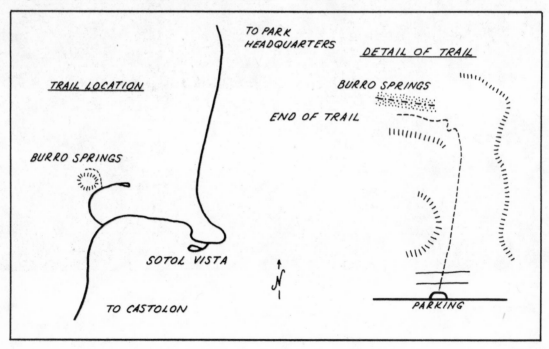

TO PARK HEADQUARTERS

DETAIL OF TRAIL

TRAIL LOCATION

BURRO SPRINGS

END OF TRAIL

BURRO SPRINGS

SOTOL VISTA

N

TO CASTOLON

PARKING

Burro Spring — with Chimneys in the distance

Distance — 2.1 Miles Round Trip
Time — 2 Hours
Elevation Change — Moderate

The Red Rocks are a group of slim, red spires that stand near the confluence of two desert washes. From headquarters, drive west 13.2 miles, then proceed south on the Castolon Road for 7.8 miles to the Blue Creek Overlook on the left (signed).

Walk the old road into the canyon bottom and over to the abandoned stone house. The house itself is worth a few minutes of your time. It was once a line cabin on the Homer Wilson ranch, and artifacts of ranching days are scattered about the house and yard.

The trail continues from the porch behind the house and passes to the left of an old corral. Just beyond the corral, on the left, is an old tank that must have been used to dip cattle. Rainwater collects in the bottom, and we saw quite a few birds taking advantage of the temporary water. If you approach the tank quietly in the early morning or early evening, and if there is water in it, you may be able to see some of the other animals that come down to drink — javelinas, rabbits, coyotes.

Just beyond the tank there is a sign which says "Blue Creek Trail." The first part of this hike is along the Blue Creek Trail which is 5.5 miles long and comes out near Laguna Meadow in the Chisos. About 0.2 mile beyond the house is a large cairn sprouting a white stake with a yellow arrow. The stake directs you up the wash for 0.1 mile, then you swing out on the right and climb a bit to reach the red rocks.

At the 1.0-mile mark, Blue Creek Trail continues on up the wash to the right — and the spires are about 300 feet off the trail on your left. Their reddish color is due to oxidized iron in the rock, and thorny desert plants crowd around their bases.

For a little variety, follow the sandy wash back down to the ranch. It hosts desertwillows, mountain buckeye (big, three-lobed pods which are poisonous) and catclaw.

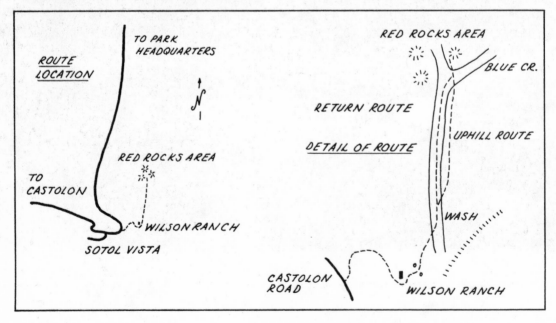

Red Rocks

13   THE CHIMNEYS

Distance — 4.7 Miles Round Trip
Time — 3 Hours
Elevation Change — Little

The Chimneys is a part of an igneous dike that has largely eroded away, leaving a line of rock outcroppings that resemble (of course) chimneys. They are a prominent landmark in this part of Big Bend, and the early nomadic hunters and gatherers were drawn to them. The Indians left petroglyphs to tell of their passing. In the more recent past, herders left signs of their passing, too — an earthen dam, windbreaks rocked into hollows at the base of the chimneys, an old corral.

From park headquarters, proceed west 13.2 miles to Castolon Road. Then proceed south 12.8 miles, and watch for a white stake with a yellow top on the right side of the road. There is no place to park at this point, but there is a pulloff about 0.4 mile north. Expect you will have to find the stake first, then go back and park. Part of The Chimneys is visible from the road.

Most of the route is gradually downhill. The vegetation is pretty typical of the Chihuahuan desert — lechuguilla, ocotillo, Torrey yucca, fluffgrass, chinograss, creosotebush. The trail is actually an old road that has overgrown and softened with age.

At the 1.5-mile mark, the trail is a bit obscure where it crosses a wash. You can see your destination, and cairns should enable you to get oriented. As you approach the chimneys, the trail passes (and comes to an end) between the larger and smaller dike formations. As you stand between the two formations, the petroglyphs and a rock shelter are at the base of the chimney on the left; the corral lies behind the chimney on your right; and, at the base of this same chimney, there is a miniature arch that resembles a doughnut or the handle on a coffee cup. The earthen dam is situated behind and beyond the left chimney. It's an interesting area, worth poking about for a while before returning by the same route.

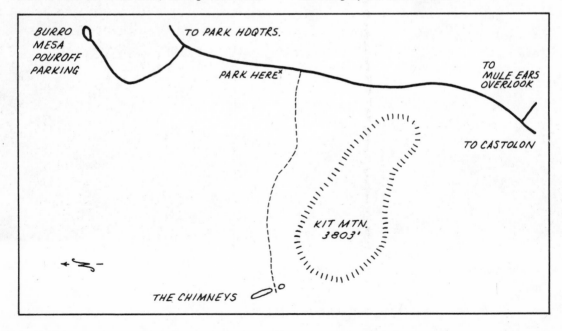

Small arch at base of a chimney

MARCH 1978
WITH MARY, MIKE HILGER,
JIM DAWES, CLEE.
EARLY MORNING, BEAUTIFUL

Distance — 1.7 Miles Round Trip
Time — 1.5 Hours
Elevation Change — Little

At one time, the Rio Grande was a much bigger river than it is today. Through millenia, as it swept in a great arc, it carved three beautiful canyons of immense proportions: Boquillas, Mariscal and — Santa Elena.

While most of Big Bend bakes in the sun day after day, Santa Elena seems to have attracted all the shade that is missing from the rest of the park. Because of the very high canyon walls, sunlight usually strikes the walls for only an hour or two after sunrise during the summer; in winter sunshine enters only as the afternoon wanes. (Photographers take note.)

From Castolon, drive west 8.2 miles to the trailhead, which is well marked. A big mesquite thicket gets the hike off to a pleasant start; then you cross the wide bed of Terlingua Creek. Terlingua's cottonwoods fell prey to man and are gone. The trail comes out of the creekbed near the mouth of Santa Elena Canyon and is shaded by mesquites and tamarisks (salt cedar). Pocket gopher mounds poke up here and there.

When you have come 0.2 mile, a series of cement ramps and steps takes you up for about another 0.1 mile to a little promontory above the river. Interpretive signs name some of the plant denizens — blind pricklypear, lechuguilla, hechtia and ocotillo. Marine fossils are sandwiched in the layers of sedimentary rock.

The concrete ends at the promontory, and the trail moves levelly above the river for a short distance before a few switchbacks deliver you to the flood plain below. You have come a little more than 0.5 mile. Common reed rustles in the breeze; and tree tobacco, with its gray-green leaves and yellow flowers, attracts hummingbirds. To really appreciate the forces of time and a river, tilt your head back and let your eye travel up the cliff beside you.

The rest of the hike parallels the river. Longnose gar, blue catfish, carp and turtles live in the river, and swallows' nests freckle the overhangs.

At about the 0.8-mile mark, the trail ends on a sandy little beach that drops off into the river. As you return by the same route, we think you'll agree that what the Santa Elena hike lacks in length it makes up for in atmosphere and scenery.

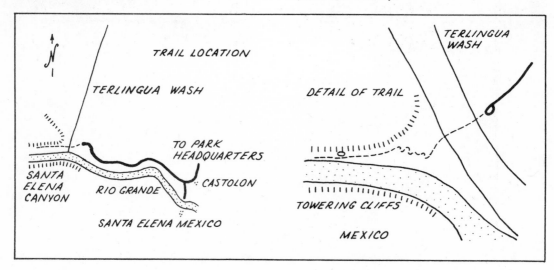

Santa Elena Canyon

15 NORTH RIDGE

Distance — 7.2 Miles Round Trip
Time — 6 Hours
Elevation Change — Moderate

The Davis Mountains attain an altitude of a little over 8,000 feet and are a range of rolling hills and long, bony ridges. Their contours are softened by tall, waving grass and spiked with yuccas, sotol, oaks and junipers.

To reach the trailhead, take Highway 118 northwest from the town of Fort Davis for about 4.2 miles to the entrance to Davis Mountains State Park. Turn left, and proceed on the main park road for a little over 0.4 mile, then turn left at the intersection. Just over 0.2 mile further, turn right into the parking lot at the interpretive center. The trail is signed and takes off on the left side of the interpretive center.

The first 500 feet is very steep as the trail moves directly up the flank of the ridge. Then it levels off as it curves around above the amphitheater. From here, a series of about a dozen long, businesslike switchbacks boosts you to the top of the ridge at about 0.8 mile. When you have come 1.0 mile, the trail has skirted a little knob on the left and sets out along the basalt back of the ridge. While the trail keeps to the left side of the ridge, there is

an expansive view of the state park below, McDonald Observatory in the distance, and Limpia Canyon ahead.

At 1.2 miles, keep to the left where another track comes in and then out on the right. At 1.4 miles, the trail passes a shelter situated on Skyline Drive and continues along the ridge. Unfortunately, the trail and the road share the ridge, and at 1.5 miles, the trail crosses the paved road. Three hundred feet beyond, it crosses a fence. At 1.6 miles, keep left at a fork in the trail. There is a picnic ground above the trail at 2.0 miles, and you soon cross the road again. Beyond here, the trail joins and follows to the right along a two-track road for a short distance to a point where a sign indicates where the trail leaves the road on the right. There appears to be a trail going straight ahead, but cut up the bank to the right where the trail again takes off along the high ground.

At 2.9 miles, you cross the fence between the state park and Fort Davis National Historic Site and begin to trend downridge to a junction with Hospital Canyon Trail (see Hike 17) at about 3.2 miles. Continue straight for another 0.4 mile, and turn right where this trail tees into Tall Grass Nature Trail (see Hike 16). It is less than 0.1 mile to the overlook above the restoration of Fort Davis — and just about 3.6 miles back the way you came.

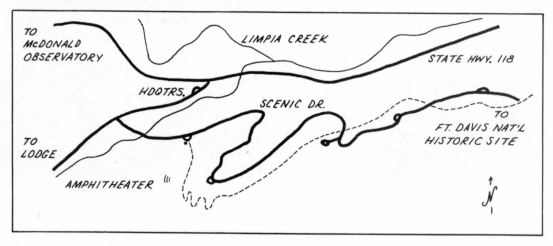

Small arch at base of a chimney

14 SANTA ELENA CANYON

Distance — 1.7 Miles Round Trip
Time — 1.5 Hours
Elevation Change — Little

At one time, the Rio Grande was a much bigger river than it is today. Through millenia, as it swept in a great arc, it carved three beautiful canyons of immense proportions: Boquillas, Mariscal and — Santa Elena.

While most of Big Bend bakes in the sun day after day, Santa Elena seems to have attracted all the shade that is missing from the rest of the park. Because of the very high canyon walls, sunlight usually strikes the walls for only an hour or two after sunrise during the summer; in winter sunshine enters only as the afternoon wanes. (Photographers take note.)

From Castolon, drive west 8.2 miles to the trailhead, which is well marked. A big mesquite thicket gets the hike off to a pleasant start; then you cross the wide bed of Terlingua Creek. Terlingua's cottonwoods fell prey to man and are gone. The trail comes out of the creekbed near the mouth of Santa Elena Canyon and is shaded by mesquites and tamarisks (salt cedar). Pocket gopher mounds poke up here and there.

When you have come 0.2 mile, a series of cement ramps and steps takes you up for about another 0.1 mile to a little promontory above the river. Interpretive signs name some of the plant denizens — blind pricklypear, lechuguilla, hechtia and ocotillo. Marine fossils are sandwiched in the layers of sedimentary rock.

The concrete ends at the promontory, and the trail moves levelly above the river for a short distance before a few switchbacks deliver you to the flood plain below. You have come a little more than 0.5 mile. Common reed rustles in the breeze; and tree tobacco, with its gray-green leaves and yellow flowers, attracts hummingbirds. To really appreciate the forces of time and a river, tilt your head back and let your eye travel up the cliff beside you.

The rest of the hike parallels the river. Longnose gar, blue catfish, carp and turtles live in the river, and swallows' nests freckle the overhangs.

At about the 0.8-mile mark, the trail ends on a sandy little beach that drops off into the river. As you return by the same route, we think you'll agree that what the Santa Elena hike lacks in length it makes up for in atmosphere and scenery.

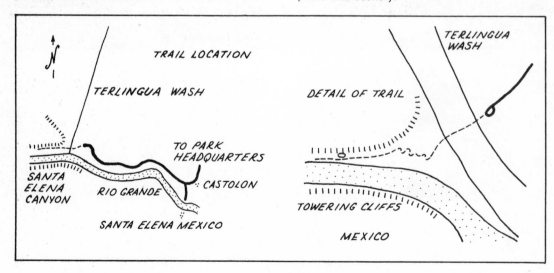

Santa Elena Canyon

15   NORTH RIDGE

Distance — 7.2 Miles Round Trip
Time — 6 Hours
Elevation Change — Moderate

The Davis Mountains attain an altitude of a little over 8,000 feet and are a range of rolling hills and long, bony ridges. Their contours are softened by tall, waving grass and spiked with yuccas, sotol, oaks and junipers.

To reach the trailhead, take Highway 118 northwest from the town of Fort Davis for about 4.2 miles to the entrance to Davis Mountains State Park. Turn left, and proceed on the main park road for a little over 0.4 mile, then turn left at the intersection. Just over 0.2 mile further, turn right into the parking lot at the interpretive center. The trail is signed and takes off on the left side of the interpretive center.

The first 500 feet is very steep as the trail moves directly up the flank of the ridge. Then it levels off as it curves around above the amphitheater. From here, a series of about a dozen long, businesslike switchbacks boosts you to the top of the ridge at about 0.8 mile. When you have come 1.0 mile, the trail has skirted a little knob on the left and sets out along the basalt back of the ridge. While the trail keeps to the left side of the ridge, there is

an expansive view of the state park below, McDonald Observatory in the distance, and Limpia Canyon ahead.

At 1.2 miles, keep to the left where another track comes in and then out on the right. At 1.4 miles, the trail passes a shelter situated on Skyline Drive and continues along the ridge. Unfortunately, the trail and the road share the ridge, and at 1.5 miles, the trail crosses the paved road. Three hundred feet beyond, it crosses a fence. At 1.6 miles, keep left at a fork in the trail. There is a picnic ground above the trail at 2.0 miles, and you soon cross the road again. Beyond here, the trail joins and follows to the right along a two-track road for a short distance to a point where a sign indicates where the trail leaves the road on the right. There appears to be a trail going straight ahead, but cut up the bank to the right where the trail again takes off along the high ground.

At 2.9 miles, you cross the fence between the state park and Fort Davis National Historic Site and begin to trend downridge to a junction with Hospital Canyon Trail (see Hike 17) at about 3.2 miles. Continue straight for another 0.4 mile, and turn right where this trail tees into Tall Grass Nature Trail (see Hike 16). It is less than 0.1 mile to the overlook above the restoration of Fort Davis — and just about 3.6 miles back the way you came.

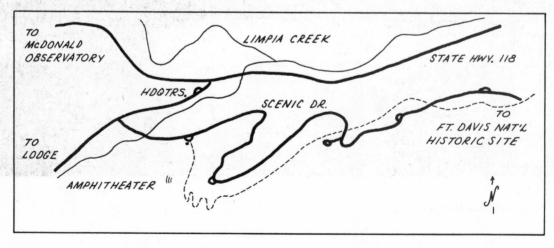

Limpia Canyon and Davis Mountains

Distance — 3.0 Miles Round Trip
Time — 4 Hours
Elevation Change — Moderate

This hike through the dunes follows a highly variable route because the terrain changes from day to day. It is a short hike, but clambering over the dunes is a strenuous business of two steps forward and one back on a shifty footing of soft sand.

Monahans Sandhills State Park is located just east of the town of Monahans along Highway 80. From the headquarters building located 0.1 mile off the highway, proceed on the main park road for 1.1 miles. At this point, a road goes right to a picnic area; but continue straight for another 0.2 mile to another fork. Keep right here for about 0.1 mile to road's end. An old windmill on the left side of the road is a favorite haunt of white-necked ravens.

From here, select your own route. (A suggested hike is shown on the map.) Try to get an early start, and avoid the area of the dunes set aside for motor vehicles. Climb a tall dune at the start in order to orient yourself. You will see a silver oil tank in the distance and should plan to turn around well before you reach it. A hike of about 1.5 miles out, plus the return hike by the same route, should be enough to make you acquainted with the dunes and some of their unique inhabitants.

Caution: Do not hike on a day when the wind is blowing as it will erase your tracks almost instantly. On a very windy day, blowing sand could also obscure your general route.

The unstable dunes at the beginning of the hike are barren and continually changing. But if you get that early morning start we mentioned, you will find evidence of a bustling nocturnal life recorded in the damp sand. This hike provides an excellent opportunity to study distinct tracks made by the local lodgers — Ord's kangaroo rats, white-throated wood rats, grasshopper mice, white-footed mice, cottontails, black-tailed jackrabbits and coyotes. Other patterns are left by the passing of bull snakes, coachwhip snakes, prairie and diamondback rattlers, mole crickets and scorpions.

A number of plants are at home in the dunes, too. In contrast to the stark dunes of pure, drifting sand at the beginning of the hike, you will cross dunes which have begun to stabilize. These dunes provide toeholds for sand sage, prairie yucca and Havard's oak — a tiny, low-growing oak which produces giant acorns. Mesquite grows in pockets among the stabilized dunes, and sand reed grows in damp depressions.

For an area which appears so sterile and inhospitable at first glance, the sandhills have a lot to offer to the hiker who takes the trouble to get acquainted.

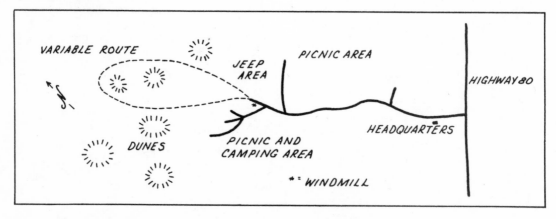

Tracks across the dunes

Distance — 6.9 Miles Round Trip
Time — 7.0 Hours
Elevation Change — Considerable

This is a loop hike utilizing the Pine Canyon Trail for the ascent, a connecting trail along the escarpment, and Bear Canyon Trail for the descent. We should mention here that if you are not a seasoned hiker or kin to a mountain goat, you should find a less direct approach to the Guadalupes.

A camping-picnicking area is located near Pine Springs along Highway 62-180 and is well signed. Pine Canyon Trail takes off from near the register at the far end of the parking area.

The first mile is gradually uphill through alligator and one-seed junipers, small oaks, sotol, nolina, soaptree yucca, dog cholla and pricklypear. The Texas madrone does well in this area, and there are a number of them along the trail — slim trunks with silver-pink bark and dark green leaves.

The next 1.3 miles is virtually straight up. The only antidote is to walk slowly, savor the expanding view, listen for canyon wrens, watch for violet-green swallows and white-throated swifts — and concentrate on one switchback at a time.

When you top the escarpment at 2.3 miles, take the right-hand trail toward "The Bowl," which soon comes up on the left. "The Bowl" is a depression which nurtures a relic forest of ponderosa pines, limber pines, Douglas firs and a few aspens — survivors of a much greater forest which grew in the area thousands of years ago when the climate was cooler and there was more rainfall. Stay on the trail. This area is very fragile and cannot withstand man's abuse. It is home to elk, mule deer, turkey and many other animals.

Just before the 2.7-mile mark, there is a fork in the trail. Keep right, and continue uphill. (Cairns mark the route in places.) When you have come 3.0 miles, a side trail goes to the right to the summit of Hunter Peak, but stay left on the main route. The short side-trip to the summit provides an excellent overall view of the park's interior.

Soon the trail trends somewhat downhill. In places, the route is a little obscure; but you can compensate by watching closely for the cairns. At 3.5 miles you reach some old water tanks, and Bear Canyon Trail heads downhill from here.

The hike down is the counterpart of the hike up — very steep. You share the route with an old waterpipe, remnant of recent ranching days. Maples and ponderosa pines accompany you part way down as the route threads among large boulders in the tight drainage.

Just before reaching the fifth mile, you swing to the right, away from the canyon. The trail fades into an old two-track road which continues down to the Bear Canyon trailhead, just beyond Mile 6.1. From here, follow the road (left) out to where it joins the road into Pine Canyon; and return by that road to the parking area.

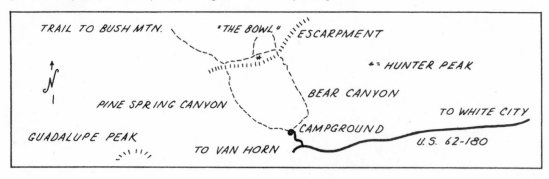

View from the escarpment

Distance — 6.2 Miles Round Trip
Time — 6 Hours
Elevation Change — Little

When the Guadalupe Mountains became a national park, the cat was out of the bag and McKittrick Canyon was on the map. It has an evanescent beauty that has made it special to veteran hikers and a handful of scientists — a fragile canyon that protects some species of plants found nowhere else in the world. For years, these plants have fought to exist in a harsh climate — and have won. For that reason, we had not planned to include McKittrick in our guide. Man could tip the scale in favor of the elements and send an entire community of unique plants over the brink. But as we traveled through Texas, we found that the increased notoriety of the Guadalupes had made McKittrick a household word. Our purpose then, since the heavy traffic is inevitable, is to inform you of the canyon's precarious place in the overall scheme so that perhaps you will treat it with extra care. Resist the temptation to wade in the pools or to traipse off the trail, and, of course, don't harm anything or litter.

At present, a shuttle bus takes hikers to the trailhead from the National Park Service information station which is located at Frijole, 1 mile east of Pine Springs (just off Highway 62-180). The canyon is subject only to day use and foot travel. We suggest you write to the Superintendent, Carlsbad Caverns National Park (address in front of guide) for current information.

The trail begins in the dry mouth of the canyon and follows the remains of an old two-track road bordered by soaptree yuccas, sotol, grasses and junipers. You cross and recross the dry creekbed until, somewhere around 1.2 miles, little pools of water begin to appear in the sand. The sides and bottoms of some are plastered with brown leaves from the oaks and velvet ashes that grow above them; others teem with green plants and minnows. In the spring, dragonflies and butterflies hover over the water, and all kinds of birds are attracted to the canyon.

When you have come about 2.0 miles, you come abreast of an old stone wall. It is worth the short walk up the path to the right to see the unusual stone architecture of the Pratt Lodge — even the roofs are of stone.

The canyon becomes increasingly pretty as the pools become larger and more frequent. Ponderosa pines line the rim and grow down the high side canyons; willows, big tooth maples, chinquapin oaks and Texas madrones shade the trail. Resurrection ferns are tucked into the landscape here and there.

Just beyond 3.0 miles, the route follows the creekbed for about 150 feet before exiting on the right. Above is a limestone overhang with stalactites and stalagmites, and just ahead is the site of the Grisham-Hunter Lodge. This is a good place to turn back if you're to catch the shuttle bus.

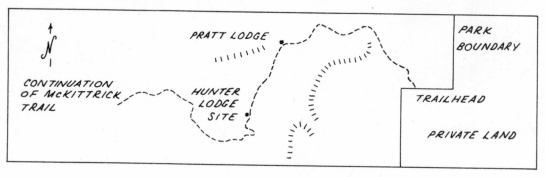

McKittrick Canyon

Distance — 3.1 Miles Round Trip
Time — 3 Hours
Elevation Change — Moderate

Desert canyons with running water or springs have a bittersweet beauty all their own, and Palo Duro has been attractive to men and animals throughout history. Most of its 120-mile sprawl through the Texas panhandle is in the firm clutch of private ownership, but Palo Duro Canyon State Park is within easy distance of Amarillo. Hiking trails are almost non-existent, but you are free to explore the rugged side canyons or to wander along the Prairie Dog Town Fork of the Red River. We selected a route up one of the side canyons just to get a classical introduction to the area. Palo Duro is sedimentary in origin, but keep in mind that on warm-weather holidays visitors are also deposited in sedimentary layers throughout the park — and time your visit accordingly.

To reach Palo Duro Canyon State Park, take Highway 217 east from Canyon for about 13 miles; or take Ranch Road 1541 south from Amarillo for about 16 miles, and then drive east on Highway 217 for about 8 miles. From the park entrance, proceed 5.4 miles on the main park road to a major fork. Turn right onto Alternate Road 5, and continue a little over 0.5 mile. Here there is a dry desert wash going under the road (metal reflector posts on each

side). There are no signs to indicate the start of the hike; it is entirely up the wash to the right. Just beyond is a little road on the right where you can pull off to park.

If you are not familiar with desert hiking, we should warn you that a storm in the canyon or on the desert above could turn this quiet drainage into a howling trough of water.

The wash is about 30 feet wide and sandy, bordered by grasses, mesquites, pricklypears, junipers and yuccas. Its banks are a colorful blend of soils and rocks — pinks, reds and rich browns, dusted here and there with white calcium carbonate crystals. If it has rained recently, the damp sand is freckled with animal tracks.

When you have come 0.6 mile from the start, a fair-sized wash joins on the right; bear left. About a hundred yards further is another fork; keep right. Near the 0.9-mile mark, the wash narrows, and the bottom is strewn with large boulders which make the going a little more difficult. Tamarisks and cottonwoods grow against a backdrop of red desert stone.

At 1.0 mile, there is a lone cottonwood growing among big boulders. The 0.6 mile between here and the end of the hike is a rock exercise requiring the use of hands and feet — and hard on equipment such as cameras and binoculars. The end comes abruptly when the box canyon dead ends at the base of a pouroff which creates a small, red amphitheater choked with big hunks of rock. The return is by the same route.

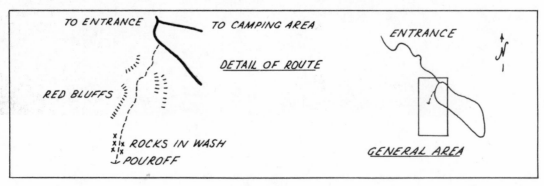

Palo Duro Canyon

22 LAKE TEXOMA HIKING TRAIL
(Cross Timbers Trail)

Distance — 14 Miles One Way
Time — One Day or More, One Way
Elevation Change — Moderate (But Often)
Topographic Maps — Denison Dam,
                    Gordonville

Denison Dam, on the Red River, was constructed between 1939 and 1944. The reservoir of water behind the dam is Lake Texoma — Texas on the south shore, Oklahoma on the north. There is a trail on the Texas shore which is 14 miles long (one way) between Juniper Point and Rock Creek Camp.

The trail was initially established by joint labors of the Sierra Club, Area Scouts and the Texoma Outdoors Club, with permission from the Corps of Engineers. The Corps has installed excellent signs and mileposts along the way to guide the hiker. Aluminum discs nailed to trees aid in finding the path, though it is so well travelled that they are not often necessary.

To reach the Juniper Point Trail Head, drive north from Whitesboro 14.2 miles on Highway 377-99 to West Juniper Point Recreation Area (if you miss the turnoff you will abruptly be on mile-long Willis Bridge, crossing Lake Texoma), which is a campground area. Turn left (west) into the recreation area and drive 0.4 mile to a fork. Keep right

and just beyond is another fork where you go left. About 0.1 mile farther is the trail head, marked with a brown and white hiker sign.

Much of the trail follows the lake shore, but there are sections of it which are routed inland through the Cross Timber forest. The lakeside portions provide vistas of the lake and shoreline far and near. Between Juniper Point and Cedar Bayou the trail frequently rises high above the lake, providing spectacular views. From Cedar Bayou to Paw Paw Point the trail wanders through the black jack oak forest, touching an occasional beach, or skirting the head of a slough. Between Paw Paw Creek Resort and Rock Creek Camp the terrain is flat, with scattered vegetation.

There are three primitive campsites off the main trail between Paw Paw Creek and Cedar Bayou. A permit is required when camping at one of these sites. Trail guides and camping permits can be obtained by writing: Resident Engineer, Denison Dam — Lake Texoma, P.O. Box A, Denison, Texas 75020.

Access to the trail at intermediate points is provided by the roads to Cedar Bayou Resort, Paw Paw Creek Resort and to Paw Paw Point. Those who camp at Eagles Roost, 5-mile Camp, or East Loop Camp, usually hike in from Cedar Bayou Resort. Those who do not wish to hike the whole trail at one time may start from any of these access points.

Shoreline of Lake Texoma

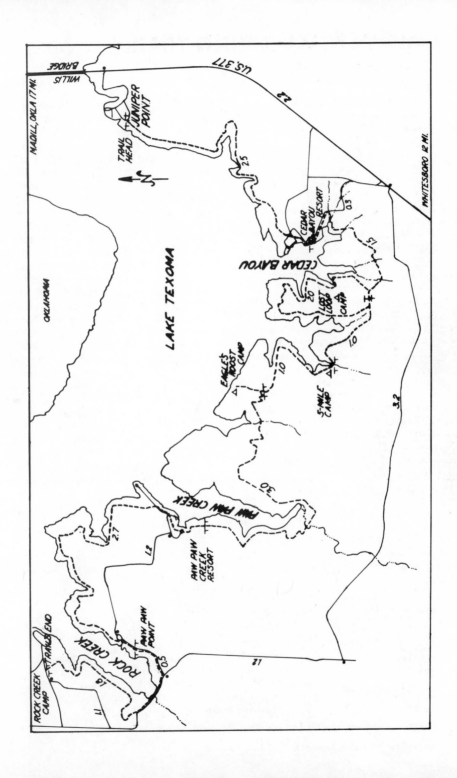

Distance — 0.6 Mile/1.8 Miles Round Trip
Time — 0.5 Hour/1 Hour
Elevation Change — Little

In 1964, Fort Worth was one of the first cities in the country to set aside some relatively unspoiled land as a natural area. Located along Upper Lake Worth, there is an interesting cross-section of natural communities — limestone cliffs, marshes, river bottoms, crosstimbers, live oak savannahs and prairies.

To reach Fort Worth Nature Center and Refuge, take Highway 199 northwest from Fort Worth, and turn right 2.0 miles beyond Lake Worth Bridge. From here, follow signs to the Robert E. Hardwicke Interpretive Center.

Caprock Nature Trail is a counter-clockwise loop which begins directly behind the interpretive center. There is a small drop in elevation which is made up on the other end of the loop. The trail is pebbled in places with limestone fossil shells, and the upper ends are shaded by oaks, ashes and redbuds. The lower stretch of trail crosses an open hillside dotted with a small species of yucca and, in spring, sprinkled with lupines and other wildflowers. Crows call down by the river on your right, and you can see a marsh which is muffled in lotus and reeds. Crickets chirp from crannies in the limestone, and we actually blundered into the midst of four young armadillos as we rounded a bend in the trail. When you have come 0.5 mile, keep left where a trail of use cuts up the hill, and continue along the caprock back to the trailhead.

Greer Island has several relatively short trails which interconnect. From the interpretive center, drive 0.3 mile back to the main refuge road, turn right, and proceed 3.5 miles to Greer Island parking area on the left. The first 0.3 mile of the hike is across the spoilbank to the island. Red-winged blackbirds sing in the willows and reeds.

When you reach the island, a sign on your left says, "Audubon Nature Trail." The trail is a sandy path through a green tunnel of vegetation and then through a sunny copse of spindly willows and cottonwoods. There are many side trails, and there's a good possibility that you will stray off onto one of them; but distances are short enough to allow for course corrections with little trouble. Keep left about 350 feet from the start where a trail enters from the right. Eight hundred feet further, take the left fork; and 100 feet beyond that, turn right at a junction. Near the 0.3-mile mark, you come to the edge of the lake on the left. A hundred or so feet from here, keep left where another trail comes in on the right. Just beyond a clearing a bit further on, keep left at a trail fork. The route passes a shelter and, when you have come 0.5 mile, you come out in a cleared area where you began the Audubon hike. Turn left here, and walk out on another spoilbank for about 0.4 mile to where it is low and wet. The bank is mulched with beer cans and bait boxes, but wood ducks, green herons, other water birds and beaver could make it a worthwhile annex to the hike.

Return along the bank, cross the clearing, and return along the first spoilbank to the trailhead.

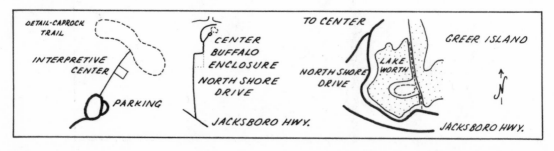

Yucca along trail

Distance — 3.4 Miles Round Trip
Time — 2.5 Hours
Elevation Change — Little

The Fort Worth Nature Center and Refuge lies in the crosstimbers — a short oak transitional forest area separating Eastern deciduous forests and Western prairies. Crosstimbers Hiking Trail follows a dirt road along the West Branch of the Trinity River and then an older road which makes a circuit through the woods.

To reach the Center, take Highway 199 northwest from Fort Worth, and turn right 2.0 miles beyond the Lake Worth Bridge. When you have come in about 0.2 mile, keep left at a fork. Another 1.1 miles further, keep left again and continue another 0.4 mile to unsigned parking beside the river on the left.

Hike along the road between the river on the right and Lotus Marsh on the left. Willows and cottonwoods grow along the banks, and fishermen have taken root here and there. When you have come just a little over 0.5 mile, turn left onto the older road. (There is a gate here.)

The road crosses a grassy area and enters the trees. About 0.2 mile beyond the gate, another more obscure road comes in on the left. Keep right here to begin a counterclockwise loop which will bring you back to this point. Sun-dappled oaks, some of which are liberally hung with wild grape, shade the trail along much of the route. At the 1.4-mile mark, there is a murky green slough on the right; and the trail begins to trend left just beyond here. The "backstretch" of the loop is overgrown, and poison ivy and nettles inspire some fancy footwork in places.

Because the trail alternates between woods and open areas, you might be able to spot deer and other wildlife before they spot you. Also, chrome-green tiger beetles seem to be quite common along the trail.

At 2.6 miles, this road joins with the first to complete the loop and you keep right to return to the trailhead.

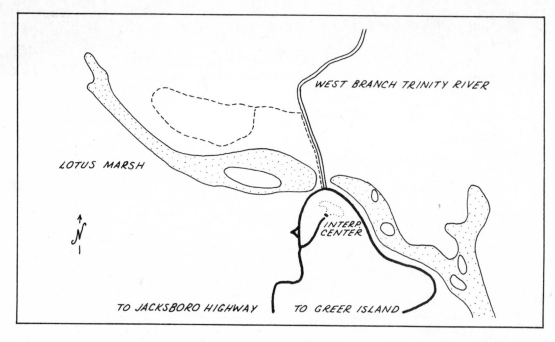

WEST BRANCH TRINITY RIVER

LOTUS MARSH

INTERP. CENTER

N

TO JACKSBORO HIGHWAY   TO GREER ISLAND

Afternoon hike through a hardwood forest

Distance — 0.8 Mile/1.1 Miles Round Trip
Time — 1 Hour/1Hour
Elevation Change — Little

Ashe juniper (or "cedar") is one of the predominant trees in Meridian State Park. While juniper is the object of an eradication program by farming and ranching operations, it is of vital importance to the golden-cheeked warbler. This is the only species of bird that breeds only in the state of Texas; and, as his habitat is rapidly being converted to fence posts and firewood, he is now an endangered species. These two short hikes are in an area where you might chance to see a golden-cheeked warbler — if you and the bird are both lucky this year.

Meridian State Park is just off Highway 22 about 2.4 miles southwest of Meridian. In addition to the two hikes described here, there is a third hike (Bosque Trail, Hike 26) around the lake.

Little Springs Nature Trail begins across the road from park headquarters. Continue straight ahead at a trail junction about 450 feet from the start of the hike. Junipers and oaks shade the trail as it drops down a little limestone cliff to another junction. Keep right here, and cross the creek. (This is the beginning of a clockwise loop.) When you have come 0.3 mile from the start, make a right across the creek. Five hundred feet further, you again cross the creek. At 0.6 mile, the trail crosses a rock catchment dam, and at 0.7 you turn right to complete the loop which joins your first trail about 250 feet beyond. Turn left here, and make the short, uphill climb to the trailhead.

The second trail goes by the ignominious name, "Little Forest Junior Trail." Designed to be an interpretive trail for children, it is actually a pleasant hike for anyone who wants a short ramble. The first and last parts of the hike are along the Bosque Trail, so see Hike 26 for directions to the trailhead.

When you have come about 700 feet up (yes, up) the Bosque Trail, you pop out on the edge of a little meadow beside an interpretive sign. This is where you begin a counter-clockwise loop by turning right on the Little Forest Junior Trail. Butterflies and bluebonnets, black-eyed Susans and bees fill the meadow in springtime.

After crossing a paved road at 0.2 mile and a 2-track road at 0.5, the trail threads along the tops of small limestone cliffs so that you are at eye level with the tops of the trees. From Bee Ledge, at 0.8 mile, you have an expansive view of Meridian Lake, and you are back on the Bosque Trail. Turn left here, and continue up to the paved road just above. Cross the road; then hike along another paved road that tees in directly ahead. About 400 feet down this road, turn left and cross the meadow back to the interpretive sign where you began the loop. From here, retrace your steps to the trailhead.

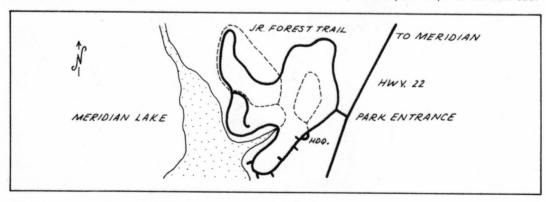

Swallowtail on thistle

Distance — 2.3 Miles Round Trip
Time — 2 Hours
Elevation Change — Little

Meridian Lake was created when the CCC built a rock and earthen dam across Bee Creek. The hilly limestone terrain is mantled with ashe juniper, post oak, blackjack oak, live oak, white oak and, in spring, wildflowers. The park is just off Highway 22 about 2.4 miles southwest of Meridian. From the park headquarters, proceed 0.2 mile on the main park road to a fork beyond the trailer camping area, and turn right. Follow this road for another 0.2 mile to a picnic area and Bosque Hiking Trail sign on the left. The sign indicates that the distance around the lake is 5.0 miles, but they're putting you on. We measured it at just over 2.3 miles.

The trail begins directly across the road and climbs for the first 700 feet to an interpretive sign on the edge of a meadow. Along this part of the hike, a short distance in from the road, is a spur going right to Little Springs Trail (see Hike 25), but keep left. At the interpretive sign, keep left again. The right fork is the Little Forest Junior Trail (see Hike 25). Across the meadow is a paved road which you follow to the right for about 400 feet to where it tees in with another paved road. Cross the second road, and take up the trail on the far side. When you have come just over 0.3 mile, you come out on a limestone outcropping above the lake which is called Bee Ledge, the nesting place for a colony of honeybees.

At the far end of the ledge, take the lefthand trail which drops down limestone steps to another ledge where it turns right and continues for a short distance before dropping down to the lake. We passed some time here watching turtles sunning themselves on a snag in the lake. About 900 feet beyond the Bee Ledge, you pass through a pretty area of backwaters and cedar bridges shaded by dense stands of deciduous trees. Continuing around the lake, there is a spot where the trail climbs a little before dropping back down to the lake.

If you do much hiking in East Texas, you are going to encounter bushels of armadillos — such as the four we saw on the Bosque Trail. The female always bears identical quadruplets so that the young are often found in groups of four. These four were so intent on rummaging that we were able to infiltrate their ranks before they became aware of us. Then they seemed a little confused — rising up on their hind legs to stare up at us with mild, myopic alarm. They finally came to the conclusion that something was amiss and went bouncing and barging into the underbrush.

About 1.2 miles from the start, cut directly across a small parking-picnic area, and take up the trail on the other side. Seven hundred feet further, the trail mingles with an old road beneath cottonwoods. This soon joins a well-used dirt road. Follow the road left for about 300 feet (crossing a bridge) before dropping off on the left to return to the water's edge.

Cross the dam at 1.8 miles, then trend left along the beach between bathers and buildings, then continue through the picnic ground to the trailhead.

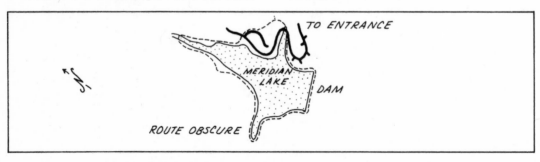

Armadillos — identical quadruplets

Distance — 0.9 Mile Round Trip
Time — 1 Hour
Elevation Change — Moderate

This area along the Paluxy River is best known for the fossil dinosaur tracks which are scattered here and there. Tracks of Pleurocelus, a 70-foot sauropod, and the upright Acrocanthosaurus can be found at several well-signed spots in the area.

The original tracks were made in mud. Water brought in sand and silt, covering them. Later, a sea covered the area, and limestone layers covered the tracks. Now the Paluxy River has eroded away the limestone, exposing the tracks. Some of these are very large; catfish often get stranded in them when the river falls.

The tracks are protected by law. Articles have been written about them in national magazines. There was an attempt a few years ago to have the area designated as the Dinosaur Trail National Monument.

The short hike described here goes to a promontory which commands a view of the park and surrounding countryside.

To reach Dinosaur Valley State Park, take Park Road 59 in Glen Rose and proceed 3.5 miles to the park entrance. To reach the trailhead, drive past the headquarters (0.2 mile from the entrance) and turn left where a sign indicates "Dinosaur Tracks" (0.2 mile beyond headquarters). A short distance ahead, turn right onto a dirt road, and continue 0.1 mile to where you turn left on a one-way loop road. 0.1 mile brings you to the tracks exhibited beside the river below on the left; another 0.1 mile brings you to parking and the trailhead for this hike.

The route is well marked. From the parking lot, drop down and cross the river. Soon after you climb the stairs on the other side, the trail crosses a grassy area and begins to climb the 0.3 mile to the top. Ashe junipers and oaks shade the trail, and the river is below on the right until (about 0.1 mile beyond the grassy area) the trail swings left away from the river and switches around back to the top of the ridge. Return by the same route.

Since we visited the area, an additional trail has been added. It is marked as a dotted line on the map.

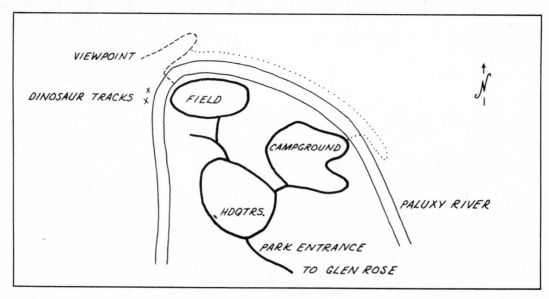

Dinosaur track

Distance — 1.0 Mile/1.9 Miles Round Trip
Time — 1 Hour/1.5 Hours
Elevation Change — Little

Lyndon B. Johnson State Park was created more for historical purposes than for outdoor recreation, so the two short hikes described here are not in an entirely natural setting. Still, it is not entirely un-natural, and you do get a sampling of Hill Country vistas and history which are interesting in themselves.

The state park is located just off Highway 290 between Fredericksburg and Johnson City. The trail leaves from the visitor center compound and crosses a grassy rise (which is blanketed with bluebonnets in spring) to a viewpoint which looks across the Pedernales River to LBJ Ranch. From here, the route angles to the right and back to cross a little creek bordered by pecans and wild grape. Not far beyond the creek crossing is a wildflower exhibit; then the trail skirts several old buildings which were once the Sauer homestead. When you reach a point where the buffalo enclosure is above on your right and the trail turns across the creek on your left, you can continue straight for a short distance to a viewpoint above the Pedernales River — or you can turn left and continue the hike. Beyond the creek, the trail borders a wildlife enclosure on the right which corrals longhorn cattle, white-tailed deer and wild turkey. The mesquites grow thickly here, and (in spring) the ground is carpeted with pink primroses. After following two sides of the enclosure, turn left and walk back to the visitor center.

The second hike is a little longer and is in a similar hiking environment. The trail had not been developed at the time we visited the park, but we walked the staked route. Start at the same place as the first hike, and share the first 140 feet; then veer left across an open, grassy area and into an old peach orchard. When you have come about 0.2 mile, the trail splits and you take the left fork which follows the wildlife fence (no wildlife in residence at the time of our hike). Shortly beyond where the trail leaves the fence, there is a weathered "dogtrot" cabin which was built by German immigrants in about 1880 and still occupied by their descendents in 1966. The building materials were post oak chinked with field stone, and it probably has more good years left to it than most houses being built today.

From here, the trail passes the swimming pool complex, crosses the road and the creek, and, at about 1.1 miles, swings right along the Pedernales River. The sloping, grassy bank and the tall trees contribute to the park-like atmosphere of the hike. At 1.5 miles there is a spillway on the river; and, at a little over 1.6, the trail climbs the slope above the river and crosses the road to re-enter the peach orchard. The loop joins at about 1.7 miles, and you turn left back to the visitor center.

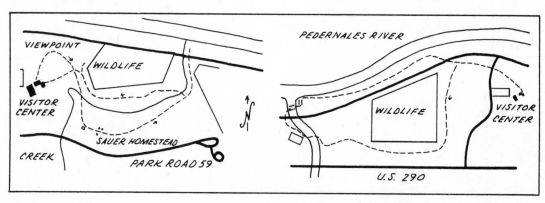

Along LBJ Trail

Distance — 8.3 Miles Round Trip
Time — 6 Hours
Elevation Change — Moderate

Dawn is the time to hike in the Hill Country — when the junipers are backlit and the birds are just beginning to stir. And the Wolf Mountain Trail in Pedernales Falls State Park is easy to follow in the half-light when deer still browse and poor wills are calling a last few times. Backpacking is permitted in an area of the park situated along the Pedernales River between Mescal and Tobacco Creeks, about 2.5 miles from the trailhead.

To reach Pedernales Falls State Park, head east on Farm Road 2766 for 9.2 miles from its junction with Highway 281 in Johnson City. Turn left into the park, and continue 2.9 miles to where a sign says, "Primitive Camping Parking Area." The signed trail takes off from the parking area.

The route sets out along a two-track road, alternately climbing and dropping. It crosses several little creeks, the first of any consequence being Bee Creek which is about 1.0 mile from the start. Last night's animal tracks mingle with the tracks of yesterday's hikers. Just after crossing Bee Creek, keep left and continue on the two-track road. When you have come about 1.9 miles, the trail crosses Mescal Creek. If you aren't backpacking, you may want to detour over to see the river; the trail continues ahead on the road. Just beyond Mescal Creek, another two-track road comes in on the right. Keep left here to begin a loop. You pass the Wolf Ridge Primitive Camp and then cross Tobacco Creek. Near the 3.1-mile mark, the left fork goes ahead to Jones Spring; but keep to the grassy track which goes right. An old rock wall rambles through the area between here and 3.4 miles where you leave the road on the right to follow a little creek.

This is the best part of the hike — a narrow brown path through the creek bottom where rufous-sided towhees scuff in the dry banks of leaves and ruby-crowned kinglets flit in the bushes. White-topped posts mark the route. There is a lot of velvety, downed wood in the area; and in one place there is a huge oak growing on the right side of the trail which has a pricklypear cactus growing in its lowest branch about 25 feet above the ground. Eventually the trail switchbacks away from the creek bottom through dry juniper and oak on the hillside and ties into the road near the 4.4-mile mark. You turn right here and, not far beyond, right again where you tee into another road. There are sweeping views of the surrounding hills as the route swings around Wolf Mountain, and you can catch occasional glimpses of the river. When you have come about 5.0 miles, keep right at a third road junction. The loop joins at 6.4 miles. Turn left and retrace your steps to the trailhead.

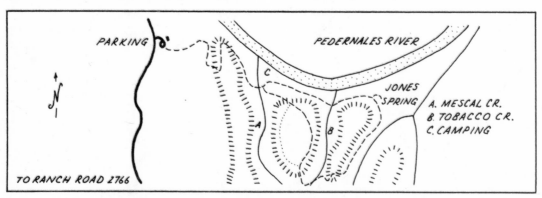

Bee Creek

Distance — 0.3 Mile/0.7 Mile Round Trip
Time — 0.5 Hour/0.5 Hour
Elevation Change — Little

The area was once known as Ottine Swamp and has long been known for its dwarf palmettos, peat bogs, warm springs and mud boils. Now, little of the old swamp remains outside of this small remnant preserved at Palmetto State Park. The two hikes described here are very short, self-guiding trails; but the area is so unique that it is worth not only the time to make the hikes but an overnight stay in spring to see the fireflies come out in the evening and to hear the barred owl calling, the frogs clicking and quacking and the neighborhood hounds baying. In the early morning, you can hear a flock of crows scolding and a dozen birds calling. Perhaps because the area is swampy and snakey, we found that it was not too crowded. Shoes for everyone and close supervision for children and pets should compensate for the "critters" which are part and parcel of a swamp.

To reach Palmetto State Park, take Highway 183 southeast from Luling about 6.2 miles, and turn right on Park Road 11. Or, take Highway 183 northwest from Gonzales for about 10 miles, and turn left on Park Road 11. Headquarters is approximately 2.1 miles in on the park road, and you may want to stop there to get copies of the trail guides for both the Palmetto Trail and the San Marcos River Trail. Continue on the main park road (Park Road 11 North) for about 0.8 mile, and turn left onto another Park Road 11. A little more than 0.4 mile along this road is the Palmetto Trail on the right.

This trail makes a lefthand loop through a dense thicket of tall trees, ropey vines, spiky palmettos and a landscape dotted with frothy green or murky black pools. A hydraulic ram pump beside the trail near the outset draws water from an artesian well to sustain the swamp. Otherwise, it would gradually disappear as the swamplands outside the park are drained and made to serve man.

When you have come about 500 feet, keep left. Toward the mid-point of the trail, the swamp borders a small meadow where mats of wildflowers bloom in spring. Wild iris and water hyacinth grow where there are little ponds beside the trail, and a stream runs through the area which is crossed via rustic bridges. The pungent odor of wild onions and decaying vegetation give the olfactory sensation of walking through a large salad.

The San Marcos River Trail takes off from the left side of the same road a little more than 0.2 mile beyond the Palmetto Trail. The river trail, for the most part, parallels the sluggish, gray-green San Marcos River which is said to give up catfish of magnificent proportions. Belted kingfishers work its surface; turtles sun on its banks. At 0.2 mile, keep right to begin a counter-clockwise loop which takes you through a stretch of dense woods. The return part of the loop is again along the river and, at about 0.5 mile, rejoins the original trail back to the trailhead.

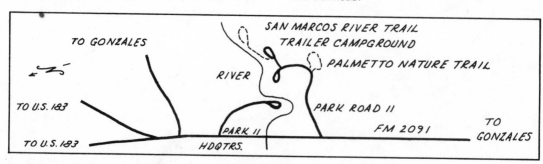

Palmetto Trail

Distance 0.9/6.0 Miles Round Trip
Time — 1 Hour/5 Hours
Elevation Change — Very Little

Padre is a barrier island — a creation of the wind and waves and still subject to their domineering whims. Here within easy reach of Corpus Christi lies 113 miles of sand, shells, sea oats and wildindigo. The width of the island varies from several hundred yards to about 3 miles. The sandy beaches on the gulf side give rise to a series of dunes which, in turn, fade into grass flats. Then there is an area of mud flats near the waters of Laguna Madre, the shallow body of water that separates the island from the mainland.

Because of its delicate ecological balance, Padre Island should be regarded as more than a place to race a dune buggy and cultivate a suntan. It is a place to wander and woolgather and to watch the constant changes taking place as weather and water do their work. Beaches and crowds are synonymous, so you may want to plan your visit accordingly — weekdays and winter are on your side.

If you hike the Grasslands Trail as a prelude to the beach hike, you will go into the longer hike with some insights into the area. Follow signs from Corpus Christi to Padre Island National Seashore. 1.4 miles from the entrance sign is the parking area for Grasslands Trail. It is a clockwise loop 0.9 mile in length, and an interpretive leaflet is available at the trailhead. The route is laid out among the dunes which are in various stages of stabilization, and the leaflet acquaints you with some of the plants and animals that have adapted to the changeable environment of a barrier island.

For a longer hike along the beach, proceed 0.8 mile from the main park entrance and turn left. Follow the road for 0.5 mile to a parking area. Motorized vehicles are not allowed on the 3-mile stretch of beach from this parking area south to the campground. You can hike all or part of the distance, returning by the same route. Beachcombing is permitted, and the shoreline teems with birds. The abundant gulls with black heads are laughing gulls, and the comical little bird that advances and retreats with the waves is the sanderling. Willets, black-bellied plovers and ruddy turnstones wade near the shore; and three kinds of tern (least, royal and sandwich) wheel over the water or rest on the sand. The number of dead Portuguese man-of-war jellyfish that we saw on the beach prompts us to remind you to wear shoes. Even dead, they pack a powerful sting.

By now, Padre Island may have caught your fancy. If you want more than a passing acquaintance, contact a park ranger for information. Depending on the time of year and the type of vehicle you have, you can gain access to more isolated stretches of the island.

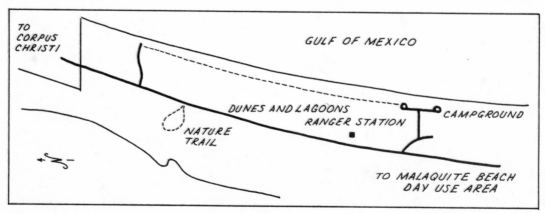

Padre seashore

Distance — 1.4 Miles/0.9 Mile/0.7 Mile
Round Trip
Time — 1.5 Hours/1 Hour/1 Hour
Elevation Change — Little

Field guides and a pair of binoculars should be standard equipment at Aransas National Wildlife Refuge — best known as the wintering ground of the endangered whooping crane. The refuge teems with wildlife. White-tailed deer are too numerous to miss, raccoons hunt along the tidal flats in the evenings, and there are several hundred species of birds, including herons, pelicans, curlews, ducks, geese, roseate spoonbills, wild turkeys and egrets. Alligators and snakes cruise the lagoons, and you could also see wild boars, coyotes and bobcats.

Several distinct types of habitats account for the large, diverse animal population. There are tidal marshes, wooded dunes, meadows and mottes, oak thickets and ponds. The three hikes on the refuge are all short, but each takes you into a different type of area. To reach the refuge, take Highway 774 off of Highway 35 and follow the signs.

Heron Flats Trail is 1.4 miles long and is located about 0.4 mile beyond the refuge headquarters. (An interpretive pamphlet is available at headquarters and contributes a lot to the hike.) The trail is a clockwise loop which takes up from the left end of the parking area as you face the gulf. The trailbed is oyster shell overlaid with mouldering oak leaves as you pass through a long thicket out to a boardwalk over a freshwater marsh. The return route skirts the tidal marshes where herons and egrets feed in the shallow water.

The Dagger Point Trail is just under 0.9 mile in length, but it takes you through the wooded dunes where the trees are low and twisted as a result of continual exposure to the gulf winds. About 2.9 miles beyond headquarters is a road to the left. Proceed 0.5 mile on this road into parking for Dagger Point. The route may be confusing as there are several other trails of use through the area. About 600 feet from the start, keep right at a junction and walk out to the point — a battered land's end where hurricanes have left only a few wind-gnarled, veteran oaks. From Dagger Point, the trail cuts back into the woods and continues gradually up to the ridge, passing a brackish dune pond on the left. From the ridge it is a short distance back to the trailhead.

Big Tree Trail is a little under 0.7 mile in length. A leaflet is available at the trailhead which is 4.5 miles beyond headquarters. In contrast to the tidal flats, thickets and wooded dunes, this hike winds through a stand of venerable old oaks — mossy bee trees with more than 400 years of history and hurricanes behind them. The clockwise loop skirts the margin of Big Tree Lake and takes you easily back to your starting point.

A stop at the observation tower and a drive over the remaining refuge road should be included in your visit to the area.

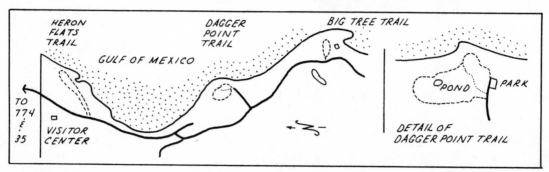

Common Egret

33 KIRBY PRIMITIVE AREA/ OLD CARTER MAINLINE

Distance — 1.6 Miles/3.2 Miles Round Trip
Time — 1.5 Hours/2 Hours
Elevation Change — Little

We have included eight hikes in this guide which are on land owned by various lumber companies. None of the hikes are arduous, and all are relatively short. All the trails have some kind of interpretation, i.e., trees are identified, pamphlets are provided, etc.

To reach the Kirby Primitive Area (owned by Kirby Lumber Company), drive north from Kountze on Highway 69-287 for 7.0 miles. Turn right on Farm Road 420, and proceed 2.9 miles to the signed trailhead which is on the left.

The first 0.7 mile is along an old road bordered by blackberry bushes. A register has been set up near the beginning of the hike. The road ends at a campsite near Village Creek where bald-knee cypress grows along the water's edge. Magnolia, longleaf pine, hickory and sweetgum shade the campsite.

The trail beyond the campsite is a little obscure. Pick it up between the water pump and the trail of use which runs alongside the creek. Flagging and painted blazes on the trees compensate for a fuzzy trail. Just before you reach the 1.0-mile point, the route skirts a slough on the left where more cypress grows. At 1.3 miles, the route is again clear and, at 1.5 miles, you cross the fence and are on the shoulder of Farm Road 420. Hike to the right

for 0.1 mile to the trailhead.

Old Carter Mainline is maintained by U.S. Plywood-Champion Paper, Inc. To reach the trailhead, turn south on Farm Road 1276 off Highway 190 between Livingston (12 miles west) and Woodville (21 miles east). Continue 1.8 miles on 1276 to parking on the left.

Near the beginning, the trail skirts a small, green pond bordered by water plants and tenanted by frogs. Straight across the pond, the route stretches along an old railroad embankment bordered by sycamores, berry vines and grass. Old Camp Ruby, an early-day logging settlement, was in this area. The tram gradually moves into the woods among yaupon, beech, sassafras, mulberry, China-berry, sugar hackberry, black gum, red oak, American holly and loblolly pine.

At 0.6 mile, turn right at a trail fork. 0.2 mile further, keep left where a road heads off to the right. At the 0.9-mile mark, you come to the start of the loop. Take the right fork here, and follow the route slightly downhill. When you have come 1.3 miles, there is a bridge across a little creek with aquatic plants, water insects and small fish.

The trail traverses a wet bottomland that may adhere to you in spots. Pecan, persimmon, cow oak, basswood, water oak, rattan, river birch and magnolia shade the trail, and cray-fish turrets poke up at frequent intervals.

The trail climbs out of the bottomland and rejoins the start of the loop at 2.3 miles. Turn right, and retrace your steps to the trailhead.

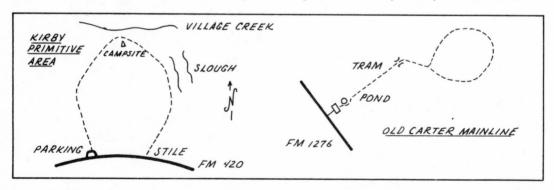

Baldcypress along Village Creek

Distance — 0.9 Mile/1.8 Miles Round Trip
Time — 1 Hour/2 Hours
Elevation Change — Little

The Moscow Trail is an attractive interpretive trail maintained by Southland Paper. Bull Creek Trail follows an exceptionally clear, spring-fed stream and is maintained by U.S. Plywood-Champion Paper, Inc.

Moscow Trail is 1.5 miles south of the town of Moscow along Highway 59. It is marked by a sign on the east side of the highway. The trail looks just the way a woodland trail should look — a well used, brown path hemmed in with hardwoods and pines and softened with last year's leaves. It bristles with interpretive signs, but herein lies the advantage to travelers who would like to know more about the area.

The route is counter-clockwise. Long King Creek runs through the area, and there are a number of rustic wooden bridges along the trail. There is a fork in the trail at 0.2 mile; keep right. At 0.6 mile you pass a piece of rusted equipment and the remains of an old road which, though last used in 1936, is still discernible. The "15-Minute Trail" comes in on the left at 0.8 mile; and, at 0.9 mile, you re-

enter the parking area to the right of where you started out. There is a register near the end of the trail.

To reach Bull Creek Trail, take Highway 287 west from Corrigan for 8.8 miles. The trailhead is on the left. At the time we made the hike, there was a "Woodland Trail" sign beside the highway, but the paper company sign appeared to have been damaged. This may have been corrected by the time you make the hike.

After passing through the fence, keep right at the fork. A small bridge takes you to the west side of Bull Creek, and the trail then keeps to the bank of the creek. Plank bridges cross tributary streams. Dark, neon damselflies flit above the water, and small fish dart over the sandy bottom. Interpretive signs name many of the trees along the trail.

When you have come just under 1.0 mile, a bridge takes you to the opposite side of the stream, and the route turns back toward the trailhead. The sandy bank of the stream is especially pretty right here. The trail back is easy and direct. Even on these very short hikes, little things dovetail into an overall good experience. This time it was a comical congregation of daddy long-legs spiders involved in a pushing and shoving competition for the shade beneath some sweetgum leaves.

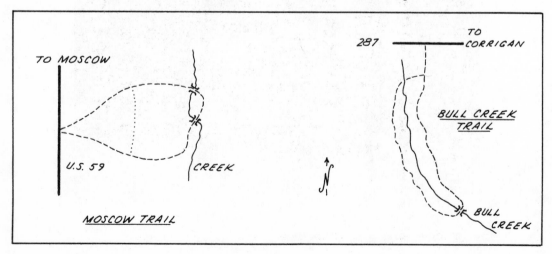

Trail through dense forest

Distance — 2.1 Miles/3.5 Miles Round Trip
Time — 2.0 Hours/3.0 Hours
Elevation Change — Little

Some of Texas' largest longleaf pines (many more than a century old) are found along the Longleaf Pine Trail which is maintained by U.S. Plywood-Champion Papers, Inc. The Dogwood Trail, maintained by International Paper Company, is in the hardwood forest where (of course) flowering dogwood flourishes. It also passes beneath some magnificent beech trees.

To reach the Longleaf Pine Trail, drive east on Highway 287 from Corrigan. When you have come 9.0 miles, turn right on Farm Road 62 and proceed 0.4 mile to the trailhead on the left. Or, you can take Farm Road 62 north from Camden for 3.4 miles to the trailhead.

The trail is a wide swath which has been mowed through the grass and other green growing things on the forest floor and is very easy to follow. There are interpretive signs on the trees. When you have come about 0.2 mile, the trail forks to form a loop; keep right. This is more of an avenue than a trail, but the open quality does afford a good opportunity to watch for birds and wildlife. Three kinds of pine grow side by side in some places — longleaf, shortleaf and loblolly. One of the birds to watch for on this hike is the red-cockaded woodpecker.

At 1.9 miles, you have completed a counterclockwise loop. Turn right and hike the short distance back to the trailhead.

To reach the Dogwood Trail, take Highway 190 east from Woodville for 3.0 miles, and turn left onto Dogwood Road. The trailhead is 0.2 mile further on the left. The main trail, which we describe here, is blazed with red paint; three other trails (blazed with other colors) break out on the right to join Dogwood Road at various points. Theuvenin Creek meanders along the left side of the trail. This is an especially good hike if you are anxious to learn the trees and shrubs of east Texas as dozens of them are identified for you — among them, American basswood, black tupelo, yaupon, swamp chestnut oak and black cherry.

When you have come about 1.6 miles, the trail skirts the left side of a good picnic site and continues straight for a little over 0.1 mile. Here it emerges from the woods near Dogwood Road. You can either retrace your steps or turn right along the road to return to the trailhead.

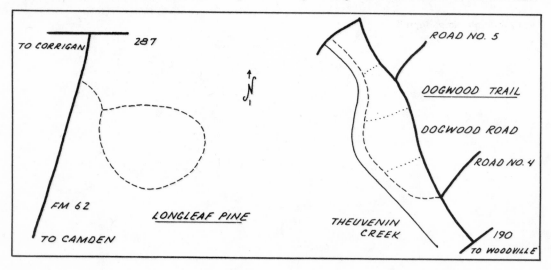

Longleaf Pine

Distance — 1.6 Miles/0.4 Mile Round Trip
Time — 1.5 Hours/0.5 Hour
Elevation Change — Little

Old River Woodland Trail is located near the historic townsite of Bevilport, once the location of a ferry for river crossings. The route follows an old logging tram for a short distance, then follows the Angelina River to a peninsula. The trail is maintained by Owens-Illinois, Inc.

Dr. Griff Ross Trail is a short walk through a very pretty wooded area. The Texas Forestry Association maintains the trail.

To reach the Old River Trail, proceed west from Jasper on Highway 190 for 8.2 miles, and turn right on Farm Road 1747. Take 1747 for 3.3 miles, and turn left on a dirt road where a sign indicates "Woodland Trail." Continue 1.9 miles to a fork, and turn right. Another 0.5 mile further, take the lefthand fork in the road, and proceed 0.3 mile to the trailhead. A guide is available here.

The trail follows the old tram through a low, damp area for about 0.2 mile, then swings right and follows the river. In addition to more than 50 plants identified in the guide, some unusual plants (spring coral root orchid, twayblade orchid, Walter's violet, toad trillium and the cut-leaved grape-fern) grow here seasonally. When you have come about 0.3 mile along the river, there is a fork in the trail which begins a loop on Old River Island; keep left here. Five hundred feet beyond, keep left again where an "alternate trail" goes right. The loop is about 0.5 mile long as it circuits the "island" formed by an ox-bow lake. When the loop joins the main trail, turn left and follow the same route back to the trailhead.

The Dr. Griff Ross Trail is located 2.2 miles east of Mt. Enterprise along Highway 84. Just beyond the fence at the trailhead, the route goes right to begin a loop. The trail crosses and recrosses a little stream bordered by honeysuckle and green briar and shaded by flowering dogwood, oaks and elms. Despite its close proximity to the highway, the deep woods has an aura of tranquility that is only accentuated by occasional highway sounds. We wished the hike were longer, but it affords an ideal opportunity for the passer-through to stretch legs and to see a pretty sampling of the country.

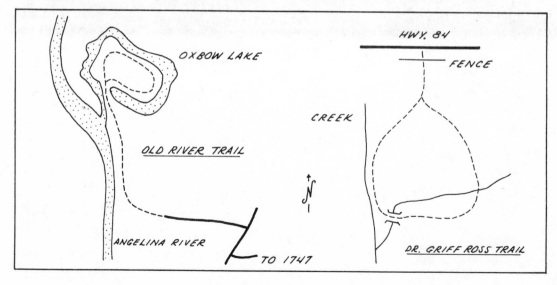

OXBOW LAKE

HWY. 84

FENCE

CREEK

OLD RIVER TRAIL

N

ANGELINA RIVER

TO 1747

DR. GRIFF ROSS TRAIL

Old wooden bridge

Distance — 2.3 Miles Round Trip
Time — 2 Hours
Elevation Change — Little

This is an interpretive trail which partially skirts a man-made lake, Lake Raven. A map, marked "Nature Trails," identifies many of the trees along the trail and is available at park headquarters.

To reach Huntsville State Park, take Interstate 45 south from Huntsville and turn right at the sign (Park Road 40). The "Botany Trail" begins on the right side of the road 0.4 mile beyond the park entrance.

About 0.2 mile in, the "Short Trail" goes right, but continue straight. The trail is wide and well defined, but it is confusing in several spots where trails of use have developed and not been blocked off. At 0.3 mile, the trail crosses a dirt road and continues straight.

When you have come 0.4 mile, keep right to begin a counter-clockwise loop. The shortleaf

and loblolly pines, sweetgum, sassafras, flowering dogwood, red maple and other trees are all typical of East Texas pine-hardwood forests. The shiny brown lizard that wriggles snake-like through the pine-needles is a skink — harmless.

At 1.0 mile is a trail junction where you keep left. After following a little creek for a way, there is a grass slough on the right where the creek runs into the lake. Crows call from the woods, and frogs croak from camouflage. As the trail meanders along the edge of Lake Raven, there are several good places from which to scan the lake for water birds.

Just before 1.8 miles, a short spur trail goes right to a parking area; keep left. Mini-bikes have obscured the route here, but about 100 feet beyond the spur trail, bear left although the main trail appears to go ahead and a trail of use comes in on the right.

When you have come about 1.9 miles, you rejoin the trail you hiked in on earlier and turn right to return to the trailhead.

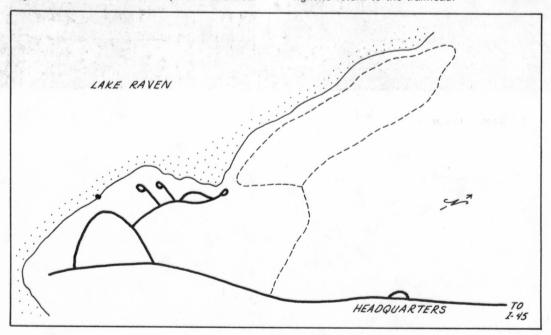

LAKE RAVEN

HEADQUARTERS   TO
                               I-45

Sweetgum leaves

Distance — 0.5 Mile Round Trip
Time — 0.5 Hour
Elevation Change — Little

The ostensible attraction of Mission Tejas State Park is a replica of a Spanish Mission to the Tejas Indians which is thought to have been established in the area about 1690. The attraction for us was the natural history of the area — a heritage which took thousands of years to develop — and a short-but-sweet trail that plays over a hillside and then drops down around a large pond. The interpretive signs along the trail are a tangible asset in a country where so many different kinds of trees and shrubs thrive — loblolly and shortleaf pine, white oak, red oak, post oak, hickory, black willow, white ash, red maple, winged elm, American holly.

Mission Tejas State Park is located in Weches, just off Highway 21. To reach the trail head, drive 0.6 mile beyond the entrance, turning right on the paved road toward the picnic area. The trail starts at the end of the road and is signed "Timber Trail."

Take the trail situated farthest right. A short climb up a path over pine needles brings you to the top of a knoll overlooking the pond on the left. At the 0.1-mile mark, keep straight where a little side trail comes in on the left. When you have come about 0.3 mile, keep right where a trail comes in on the left. The rather loud, persistent drumming that echoes through the park is the work of a large woodpecker — the pileated.

Continue around and down some stairs to a plank walk across a marshy area at the end of the pond. When you've crossed the boardwalk, turn left along the margin of the water for a short walk before crossing the dam to return to the trailhead. (This is a nice evening hike when the bullfrogs are tuning up and chuck-will's-widows call.)

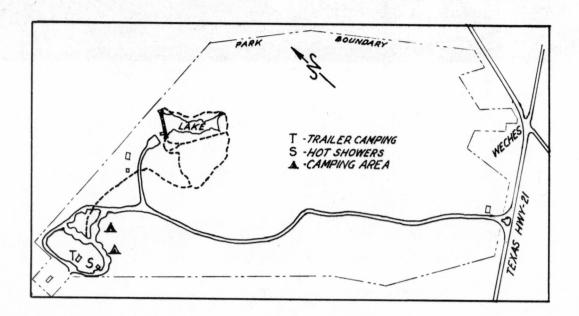

T - TRAILER CAMPING
S - HOT SHOWERS
▲ - CAMPING AREA

Forest canopy over trail

Distance — 0.8 Mile/3.3 Miles Round Trip
Time — 1 Hour/3 Hours
Elevation Change — Little

Included here are hikes in two not-too-distant state parks — Caddo Lake State Park and Daingerfield State Park. The first is an interpretive trail in an area near a big cypress bayou; the second is a trail along the lake which includes a short spur hike out to the largest chinkapin in Texas.

To reach Caddo Lake State Park, take Highway 43 northeast from Marshall, and follow signs to the park. You may want to stop at park headquarters, just inside the park entrance, to pick up the interpretive guide for the trail. We found it very worthwhile when confronted with the bewildering number of trees in the area. To reach the trail, proceed on the main park road for 0.8 mile beyond headquarters to the "Caddo Forest Trail" sign. The trail leaves the road on the right.

Downtrail about 250 feet, keep right where another trail goes left. Just before the 0.1-mile mark, there is an interesting tree on the left. Its bark is washed with green moss and has a filigree of ferns that have taken root along its trunk. The trail drops into a sandy bottomland where it mingles with a clear stream that runs in and out, above and below ground. Christmas ferns crowd along its banks, mossy logs span its narrow width, and venerable old hardwoods and cypresses shade it in warm weather. At 0.1 mile, keep left where some stairs come down

on the right.

When you have come 0.4 mile, the trail starts to climb and passes an old rock pavilion at 0.5 mile. One hundred yards beyond the building, keep right at a fork. The trail heads downhill and, at the 0.8-mile mark, completes the loop. Turn left, and return uphill to the trailhead.

Daingerfield State Park is located 2.4 miles east of Daingerfield along Highway 11-49. Turn south at the sign, and the entrance is 0.4 mile beyond. Continue on the main park road for 0.5 mile and turn right at the headquarters. Proceed 0.2 mile to a small picnic area on the left and a "Nature Trail" sign.

About 100 feet from the start, turn left at a fork. Near 0.3 mile, go left over a bridge that crosses a backwater from the lake. We saw two big turtles in the water plants below, so you might watch for turtles if the weather is warm.

The route traverses an earth and rock dam and more-or-less follows the shoreline. When you have come about 1.0 mile, turn left and walk out the side trail to see the largest Allegheny chinkapin in Texas. The 0.5-mile annex to your hike is worthwhile, not just because of the tree which is large only by chinkapin standards, but because the trail is banked with brown leaves and weaves among dense ranks of oaks and pines. There are a number of double-trunk pines in the area where you turn left to resume your hike along the main trail.

Continue following the main trail for another 0.5 mile to its end in a parking area. Return by the same route unless you want to run the gauntlet of paved roads and improvements along the rest of the shoreline.

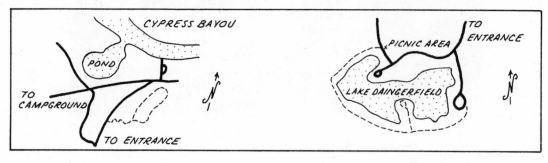

Christmas ferns growing along small creek

Distance — 3.8 Miles Round Trip
Time — 3 Hours
Elevation Change — Little

The longer the hike, the more changes of scenery and the better your chances of seeing wildlife; so we combined the two short hikes near Ratcliff Lake to give you one longer hike.

To reach Ratcliff Lake Recreation Area, take Highway 7 for 1.1 mile southwest from its junction with Farm Road 227 in Ratcliff. Turn right, and proceed 0.4 mile to parking near the swimming and concession area. The Logging Tram Trail is signed on the left side of the road just beyond the parking area.

The trail is cushioned with pine needles and the fallen leaves of hickory, flowering dog-

wood, red and white oaks. When you have walked 0.5 mile, you come out at the park road; and our version of the hike turns you left along the road for about 400 feet to where the Tall Pine Trail takes off on the left.

You cross a rustic bridge over a rusty-colored stream and continue back into the pines and hardwoods again. The creek is sluggish — banked with brown leaves that have tinted the water brown. There are several bridges along the route, and new pine seedlings crowd around old, downed trees.

There is a gate when you have come about 0.8 mile from the parking lot. Near the 1.0-mile mark, keep right at a fork; and, again, keep right at a fork near 1.5 miles. Just before 1.8 miles, you again pass through a gate, and the turnaround point is at 1.9 miles where you intercept the park road.

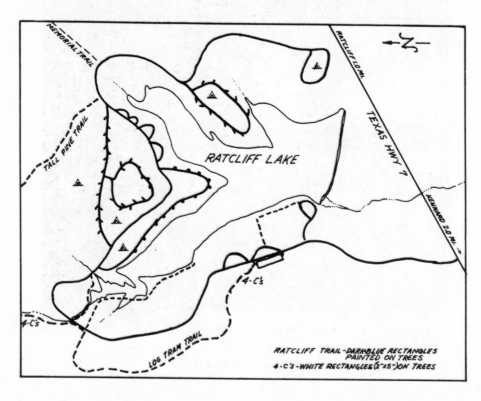

Ratcliff Trail

41 BIG SLOUGH TRAIL

Distance — 3.1 Miles Round Trip
Time — 3 Hours
Elevation Change — Little
Topographic Map — Kennard NE

The Big Slough Trail is a smooth blend of old road, old railroad tram and trail. The hike is worth the effort it takes to find the trail head. In fact, it's to the trail's credit that, after blundering around an intricate maze of back roads and arriving short-tempered and skeptical, we enjoyed the hike anyway.

From the town of Ratcliff, proceed north on Farm Road 227 for 1.0 mile; and turn right on an oiled road (Forest Service Road 547). 2.6 miles further, keep right as a road comes in on the left from behind. 0.7 mile further, keep left at junction. 1.3 miles beyond, turn right onto 519; 519-A is 0.9 mile east on 519, but continue on 519 to the trail head which is another 0.3 mile on the left. It is signed "Hikers Trail."

The first part of the route is along an old road, 519-B. About 0.3 mile down the road, you come to the first of a number of trail markers

— this one directs you to leave the road on the right. The trail has not had much use yet, but it is well enough defined that you can relax and enjoy the scenery. You soon swing left past a slough of flat, murky water. The trees stand in water, and palmettos droop beside the trail — which may be muddy and slick in places.

At the 1.1-mile mark is a trail junction; take the right fork. There is a park-like glade here where the trees are tall and widely spaced and the sun is filtered through a tall frieze of branches and leaves.

When you have come 1.8 miles, the trail tees into a two-track road that runs left along an old railroad grade hedged with blackberry brambles. It is really too hot and muggy to be hiking in east Texas the latter part of May, but you are somewhat compensated by blackberries.

After 0.4 mile along the grade, a marker indicates where the trail turns off on the right (and then immediately left). The trail continues through the woods for 0.6 mile, then swings back onto and crosses the grade. Soon after, you turn right rather than follow another trail which proceeds ahead. The trail head is about 0.3 mile farther.

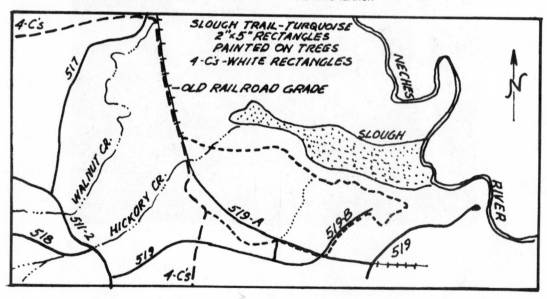

Big Slough Trail

42 FOUR-C's

Distance — 19 Miles One Way
Time — Variable, One or More Days
Elevation Change — Little
Topographic Maps — Alto, Ratcliff,
Kennard NE

The Neches Bluff Trail, which was primarily a straight line along an old logging road, is closed. A new, much more scenic trail, the Four-C's, is replacing it. The Four-C's, so named from the Central Coal and Coke Company which once logged the timber in much of the Davey Crockett National Forest, also begins (or ends) at Neches Bluff. The other end of this trail is at Ratcliff Lake.

To reach the north trail head at Neches Bluff, take Texas Highway 21 northeast from Weches (measured from the junction of Texas 21 and the road entering Mission Tejas State Park) 4.1 miles. Turn right (southeast) on Forest Service Road 511 (dirt when dry, mud when wet), and proceed 0.6 mile and turn left. The trail head is 0.4 mile down this road, on the right. Neches Overlook Campground is on this short loop road just north of the trail head.

The south end of the trail is reached by going southwest out of the town of Ratcliff about 1.1 mile on Texas Hwy. 7, from its junction with FM-227. Turn right (north) and proceed 0.4 mile to the swimming and concession area parking lot. The trail starts from the parking lot, near the concession stand.

The car shuttle is made by taking Texas 21 to FM-227, driving 227 to Texas 7 and on to the parking area at Ratcliff Lake, and returning to trail head by retracing the route to Neches Bluff.

There are 4-C trail signs marking each end of the trail (if vandals haven't destroyed them). The trail is fairly well marked with white 2" x 5" rectangles painted on trees, so it is easy to follow. The trail generally follows the routes of abandoned tramways. The trams were used for carrying logs to a sawmill which was located at Ratcliff Lake.

Much of the forest that the trail passes through has grown back since logging operations ceased in the early 1920's. The hiker enters a variety of ecosystems ranging from bottom land hardwoods to dry upland pine forests. The route crosses many streams, some of which are sparkling clear, but the water should always be treated prior to drinking it. The trail can be hiked year round, but it is much more pleasant hiking in the cooler months.

The path crosses eight roads, somewhat evenly spaced along the route, with no uncrossed section more than 5 miles long. These roads enable the hiker to start at an intermediate point and hike short sections of the trail, rather than doing it all at one time.

A trail guide and up-to-date information can be obtained by writing the U.S. Forest Service, East Loop 304, Crockett, Texas 75835. The information is also available from the Forest Service office in Ratcliff, Texas.

Four-C's

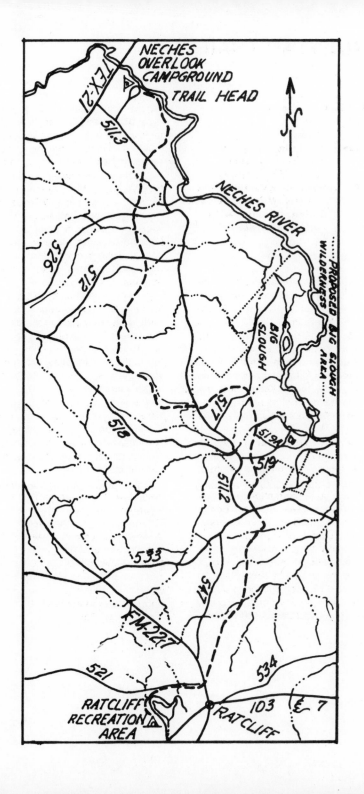

43   LONE STAR TRAIL

Distance — 140 Miles, One Way
Time — Variable
Elevation Change — Little
Topographic Maps — Richards, San Jacinto,
Montgomery, Lake
Paula, Moore Grove,
Huntsville, Phelps, New
Waverly, Maynard, Cold
Spring, Camilla, West-
cott, Bear Creek

The Lone Star Trail was originally laid out by volunteers from the Houston Group of the Sierra Club. It traverses Sam Houston National Forest and is maintained by the Sierra Club.

In reality, there is not one big, long trail as the map indicates. Theoretically, there is one long route, but further explanation is in order. Parts of the route are well marked with travel along nice, narrow paths through the forest. Other parts are along Forest Service roads, pipeline rights-of-way, even highways. Some stretches are across private property.

The Sierra Club is working diligently to keep the trail clear and well-marked, but vandals and hunters oftentimes remove trail markers or shoot them out. For this reason, it is best to hike in small parties to better keep your orientation from one marker to another in those areas where the dense foliage can make the trail hard to follow. A whistle for each hiker is very useful for signaling.

The "trail" is marked (much better in some places than in others) with aluminum rectangles (or some older triangles may still be seen) on trees. Campsites are indicated by three markers grouped on one tree. Water is available only at some places, and local inquiry should always be made in regard to its potability. (It should still be treated.)

Weather starts to cool toward the end of September, but deer season usually runs from sometime in November until the first of the year. Hiking could be risky at this time. From about the first of the year through mid-April, hiking conditions are at their best. In May, some of the less pleasant aspects of hiking in east Texas begin to intrude on your enjoyment: hot, humid weather; poison ivy, which ranges from common to abundant; ticks (tenacious); mosquitoes (voracious); redbugs (ravenous). Hiking and camping the trail from May through September is not recommended for these reasons.

Portions of the trail have been rerouted from time to time, but no additional changes in the trail routing are anticipated for the next ten years, or so. The Forest Service plans to seek National Recreation Trail status for the Lone Star Trail. Even then, the trail's maintenance will depend heavily upon volunteers.

The map shown is only a general guide. We strongly recommend that you contact the U.S. Forest Service, P.O. Box 969, Lufkin, Texas. There are also Forest Service Offices in Cleveland and New Waverly, Texas. They can provide you with a hiking trail guide which is up to date, plus other current information.

The ingredients for a first-class hiking trail exist here, but it will require more hikers and more volunteer work to turn it into a bonafide trail. Volunteers might consider contacting the Raven Work Center or the Cleveland Ranger District to see what kind of help is most needed and where.

The following hikes included in this guide are on parts of the Lone Star Trail: Little Lake Creek Loops, Stubblefield Lake, Four Notch Loop, Double Lake, Mercy Trail, Big Creek (Big Thicket), and Winter's Bayou.

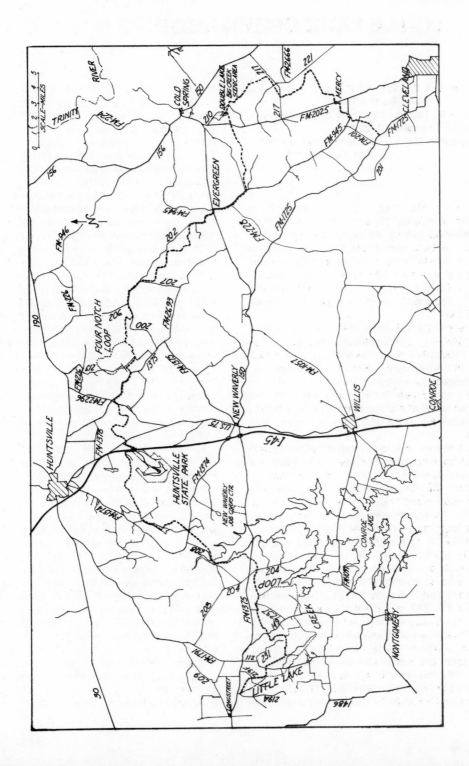

44 LITTLE LAKE CREEK LOOP

Distance — 6.3, 12.7, 19.0, 28.6
Miles Round Trip
Times — 5, 10, 15, 22 Hours Respectively
Elevation Change — Little
Topographic Maps — Richards, San Jacinto,
Montgomery

The Lone Star Trail forms one side of the multiple, elongated loops. There are three intermediate trails cutting across from the Lone Star Trail to the Little Lake Creek Trail. This makes it possible to start at the trail head and hike just about any distance you choose. An even greater choice of hikes is made possible by the roads which cut across the loops, giving access at these points too.

To reach the trail head, take I-45 south from Huntsville, or north from Houston, and go west on Farm Road 1375 near New Waverly. About 14.2 miles west, keep right where 1375 tees into Hwy. 149. Proceed northwest on 149 for 3.7 miles and turn left onto Forest Service Road 219. The trail head is located at a cattle guard 40 yards south to FM-149 on F.S. Road 219. Turn east from cattle guard.

At 0.1 mile the trail joins a two-lane vehicle path coming from the left and proceeds SE 30 yds. to a sign post. Here the main Lone Star Trail branches to the left (SE). The vehicle path and Little Lake Creek Loop branch right. To follow this write-up, take the left branch and follow the rectangular aluminum markers of the Lone Star Trail. There are Forest Service distance markers at 1, 2, 3, 4, and 8 miles on the Lone Star Trail.

The route goes around gullys, through low, wet areas, crosses ravines, and at 1.35 miles joins a poor road and proceeds SE. At 1.7 mi. the trail crosses F.S. 203, a dirt road. This provides an intermediate access to the trail. The path leads S-SE at the 2-mile marker and winds through vines to a sinkhole where it turns east. At 2.2 mi the trail turns south and crosses an abandoned pipeline. Across the pipeline it appears to widen, but abruptly turns right, then left to S-SE. Between here and the 3-mile marker the trail crosses several low,

wet depressions. At 3.1 mi. is an intersection with a crossover to the right. This is the 6.3 mile loop turnoff to the Little Lake Creek Trail. Those who wish can crossover here and return to the car. From here the trail continues east and downhill. At 3.45 mi. the route crosses F.S. 211, a gravel road (another access point) and at 3.5 mi. it follows a pipeline right-of-way to the right, (SE) for 0.2 mi. At 3.8 mi. is the 4-mile marker, and the trail returns to the pipeline ROW. The trail proceeds downhill at 4.5 mi. on a rutted road, crosses a draw and goes back uphill. At 4.8 mi. it crosses a dirt road. At 5.0 mi. the trail forks to the left and after 40 yds. comes to a clearing with a dirt road crossing it.

The intersection to the right with the second loop crossover trail to Little Lake Creek Trail comes at 5.25 miles. Continuing on the main trail, it crosses three dirt roads before joining a dirt road at 5.8 mi., and continues E-SE. At 5.95 mi. is a plank bridge over a wet area and again at 6.0 mi. it crosses a plank bridge, then turns a sharp left, then right again to NE and at 6.1 mi. joins a dirt road coming from the left. The trail crosses three dirt roads before it comes to a barbed wire fence at 6.75 mi., where it makes a sharp turn to the left and leads north along the fence. At 6.7 mi. the third crossover trail branches off to the right.

At mile marker 8.0 the trail crosses Pole Creek and heads E-NE. A clearing with new timber is crossed at 8.1 mi and at 8.2 mi. the route intersects a dirt road and turns left (N). The path forks left off the dirt road at 8.25 mi. and at 8.4 mi. crosses a fence, under a power line, and across a dirt road and on through the trees to FM-149 at 8.5 mi.

From FM-149 it continues basically a bit north of east to Osburn Road (closed) where there is parking space for several cars. From Osburn Road the trail continues east for .5 mile to its junction with Little Lake Creek Trail. The main Lone Star Trail continues east from the intersection.

Little Lake Creek Trail proceeds south and slightly east on departing the main trail and crosses a ditch on a log at .3 miles from the junction. The trail follows an old road and crosses another drainage ditch at .5 mi. If the water is high, a convenient log crossing is to the right of the trail. A few steps farther and the trail turns left into the

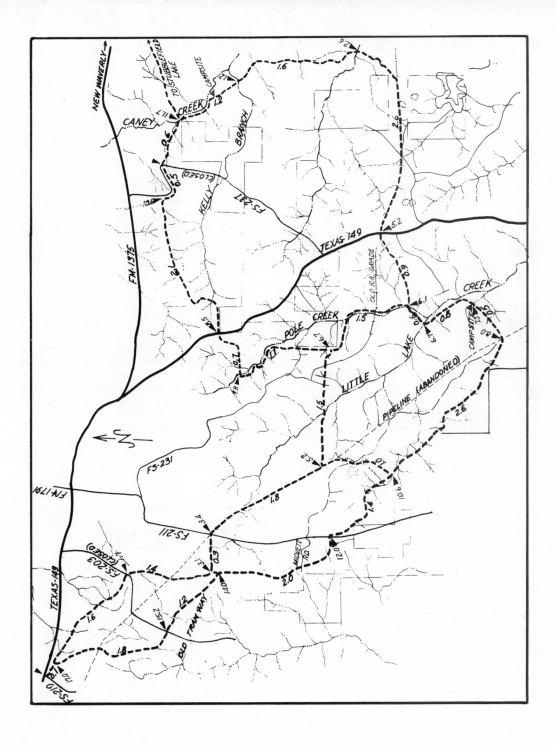

dense woods. You will be walking parallel to Caney Creek and will arrive at a couple of camping areas along the creek at .7 mi. From here the trail leads into the lowlands where hardwood trees predominate. Soon you will arrive at Kelly Branch, at 1.2 mi. At about 1.4 mi. you cross under a fallen tree, watch for deer in this area.

At 1.6 mi. and 1.8 mi. are two palmetto areas. If it is dry, you can follow the old unmarked trail on the other side. From the last palmetto area the trail proceeds, with several turns to where it splits into two trails at 2.2 mi. The trail to the right should be used in wet weather. The drier trail leads to a clear cut area at 2.3 mi. and follows the edge of the clearing to 2.5 mi. After going back into the woods, the trails join again at 2.7 mi. and arrive at another creek at 2.8 mi.

A little past the creek, on the right, is an area reported to have a giant Osage-orange tree and a honey locust tree worth looking for.

After leaving the creek the trail goes uphill, turns west and back down slightly, and at 3.1 mi. passes within 40 yards of the boundary with a section of private land. The trail goes back uphill and turns right at 3.3 mi. onto an old logging road, previously an old railroad bed. The trail goes off and on the old railroad bed and arrives at a high spot at 3.7 mi. which is occassionally used for camping. The trail crosses a ditch at 3.9 mi. and then reaches a gravel road at 4.1 mi. It crosses the road again .1 mi. farther along and continues on the railroad bed, crossing two large ditches at 4.6 and 4.9 mi. and arirves at Hwy 149 at 5.2 mi.

Where Little Lake Creek Trail crosses Hwy 149, 3.5 mi. south of F.M.-1375, there is parking for several cars. From the road, the trail continues west along the old railroad bed for .1 mi. and turns SW. It now follows along a normally dry creek bed and meanders along the creek bed and through the woods. After crossing a large ditch at 5.9 mi. it proceeds uphill to a high spot in the pines at 6..0 miles. It continues, with several turns, and arrives

at Pole Creek at 6.3 miles.

Just prior to reaching Pole Creek is a low area densely covered with canes which is sometimes difficult to get through because of the fast growth rate. About .1 mile beyond the creek (6.4 mi.) is an intersection with one of the trails cutting 1.5 mi. across to the Lone Star Trail. At 6.7 mi. the trail crosses Little Lake Creek, the namesake for this loop. The trail stays west of the creek and occasionally returns and follows along the creek bank. In dry weather the creek is dry except for some deeps where many small fish are trapped. At 7.5 mi. the trail arrives at the "Little Lake" camping area. A small lake is located here and this appears to be a popular camping area. At 8.3 miles the trail crosses Midyett Road.

About .7 mi. farther (8.9 mi.) go left along a logging road, and about .3 mi. farther you face a big fenced field, follow the road around to the right. You leave the road at 9.3 mi. (to the right). At 10.6 mi. is a junction with the crossover trail, (1.0 mi.) to the Lone Star Trail, completing the second loop. At 10.9 mi. you turn right along a fence. Keeping about parallel with the fence gets you through a congested area that has been logged; then, at 11.8 mi. you cross left over the fence (no gate, just a marker to signal you to the other side). At 12.0 mi. you cross FS-211, a dirt road. Watch closely for markers here.

At 12.2 mi. the route goes right along a cleared area for a couple hundred feet, then turns left and crosses the area. The trail junction with the crossover trail which completes the first loop with the Lone Star Trail is on the right at 14.0 mi.

Just beyond 14.0 mi. is a marshy area that has been chewed up by motor bikes. At 14.6 is an obscure area where you cross a creek with high banks. Go directly across, trending left. At 15.2 mi. you cross a two-track road, FS-203. There is a trail fork coming in from the left at 15.2 mi.; continue straight ahead. At 15.5 mi. the trail joins a road which it follows for 1.5 mi. to the trail head.

Forest floor carpeted with ferns

45   STUBBLEFIELD LAKE

Distance — 4.1 Miles Round Trip
Time — 3 Hours
Elevation Change — Little
Topographic Map — Lake Paula

This hike is along a sylvan stretch of the old Lone Star Trail, which has been rerouted. It is a brown path, well traveled and marked, that begins in the hardwood forest near the lake and ends at a logging road in a pine forest. If you are not familiar with East Texas flora, there is a leaflet available at the Raven Work Center (see "Agencies and Organizations") which identifies many of the plants along the trail.

To reach the trail head, take Interstate 45 south from Hunstville and head west on Farm Road 1375 near New Waverly. At 2.4 miles, you pass Raven Work Center; at 9.6 miles, turn right on Forest Service Road 204 toward Stubblefield Lake Campground. The trail head is marked by a sign on the left at 2.7 miles, and the campground is 0.2 mile beyond the trail head.

The footing may be damp at first as the trail crosses a marshy area dotted with pools. Little fish dart in the water, and black willows stand on the banks. Soon the path firms and is hemmed in by hardwoods. In spring and summer, red-eyed vireos call in the canopy; and Carolina chickadees, pine warblers, tufted titmice and red-bellied wood-peckers are usually busy about the neighborhood.

At the 1.6 mile mark, there is a place where the trail appears to go straight ahead parallel to a small creek on the left. Instead, turn left and cross the creek with the old trail markers. (If you do much hiking on the Lone Star Trail, you learn to feel very insecure in the presence of unadorned trees.) This part of the trail sees less use and is a little more narrow. The filtered light of the dense hardwood forest has been exchanged for the shafted light of the more open pine forest; the velvety floor of the hardwood forest has been exchanged for the pungent floor of the pine forest.

When you have come 2.0 miles, the trail passes through a gate. Less than 100 yards beyond is a logging road, and a glance at the map tells you it is possible to follow the road back to the trailhead.

An optional hike from Stubblefield Campground is on the new Lone Star Trail, following the lake shore southward. It is an hour's easy hike to where the trail leaves the lake and goes into the forest. The ground is low and somewhat swampy and there are many palmettos. The path crosses two small drainages that are only a couple of feet wide. About 1.3 to 1.8 miles, where the shoreline is some distance to the east end of the trail, there are several stands of tall pines (between trail and lake) that would make very good campsites. The trail continues through the forest to cross F.M.-1375 at 2.9 miles from Stubblefield campground.

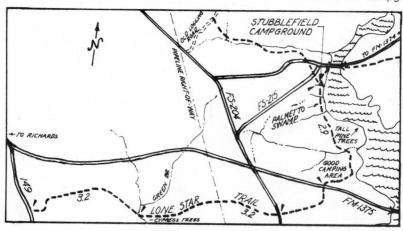

Pine seedlings and mushroom

46 FOUR NOTCH LOOP

Distance — 9.5 Miles
Time — 4 Hours
Elevation Change — Very Little
Topographic Maps — Phelps

The Four Notch Loop is a loop of a section of the Lone Star Trail. The loop has a nice campsite by Boswell Creek, near its midpoint, which makes this an easy overnight backpack trip in a beautiful mixed forest.

The trail head is at a large, cleared area where a fire tower used to be located. To get there, take Highway 190 east from Huntsville for 5.6 miles, and turn south on Farm Road 2296. Proceed 3.2 miles, and turn left onto Four Notch Road. Continue 2.4 miles southeast, then turn left, and another 0.1 mile brings you to the parking area.

An alternate approach route from I-45 is from New Waverly. From I-45 take FM 1375 east into New Waverly. Cross the railroad tracks and follow 1375 left to the end of the pavement (approx. 8 miles). Turn left for a mile, and follow the road left again for 3 miles (approx.); turn right on a dirt road, and another 0.1 mile brings you to the parking area.

Pick up the main Lone Star Trail across the road from the parking area and follow it about 0.5 mile, where the Four Notch Loop begins. Turn off, heading west on the Loop.

At .46 mile, there is a gum tree swamp on the right (east).. Here you will notice white paint on a tree, denoting that this area is designated as a sanctuary for the protection of a red-cockaded woodpecker colony. The habitat of the red-cockaded woodpecker extends throughout the Four Notch area. The trail continues, crossing some old logging roads and a number of small creeks and/or gullies, which present no problems to the hiker.

At approximately 1.8 miles, the trail turns left (north) and follows a logging road a short distance and turns off into an old bug cut. Although the trees are smaller through this area, the trail is well defined and proceeds only a short distance before leading back into an older forested area.

The trail follows along Boswell creek for a good distance. This is a particularly scenic section of the trail. At 3.6 miles is the campsite mentioned earlier — near an ancient Magnolia with moss and leathery leaves. A few palmettos grow in the vicinity.

The trail continues along the creek for a mile or so, up and down gullies and across creeks. At 4.7 miles, the route crosses a fence that encloses a plantation of about 100 acres planted in 1969. There is a clear cut at 5.3 miles which was cut in 1967. The trees are now vigorous. The loop ends at 5.62 miles, at which point it intersects with the main Lone Star Trial. Turn right to return to the parking area. It is approximately 3.9 miles.

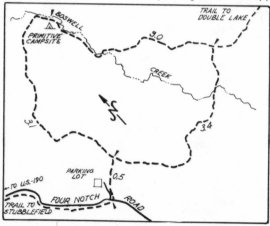

Fungus on log

Distance — 7.1 Miles Round Trip
Time — 5 Hours
Elevation Change — Little

This hike from Double Lake south to Big Creek Scenic Area is part of the Lone Star Trail. For the most part, the trail is along the banks of Big Creek; and, if it has rained recently, you can expect to muddy your feet in several low places.

Drive north on Farm Road 2025 from Cleveland for 15.6 miles to Forest Service Road 210. A sign at this junction indicates Double Lake Recreation Area, and you turn right. Proceed 0.6 mile to junction with 210-A and turn left. Proceed 0.9 mile to a sign: "Hiker Trail."

The Lakeshore Trail, which is signed on this side of the dam, is not a part of the described hike, but you may want to take it later. Hike ahead across the dam. As you come off the dam, there is a sign, "Double Lake Trail." Take the left fork here, and follow the aluminum Lone Star Trail markers. There is Spanish moss on the trees bordering the trail. After crossing a road at the 0.8-mile mark, the trail follows Big Creek.

You aren't far from the Big Thicket, and the vegetation is dense and varied. All along the trail are flowering dogwood, American holly, ferns, partridgeberry, water oak, red oak, cow oak, hawthorn. At about 1.2 miles, a side creek has tunneled beneath a large tree, and the trail crosses the creek via the exposed roots. Near 2.0 miles, the trail goes through a grove of old magnolias, and you're scuffing through banks of leathery brown leaves. The route is a little fuzzy here, but watch for the markers and keep close to the creek.

At 2.7 miles is a particularly marshy, mucky area, and the trail crosses and recrosses the creek. At 3.5 miles is a fence at the boundary of the Big Creek Scenic Area. From here, the trail into the Scenic Area goes 0.6 mile before joining the Big Creek trail (see Hike 49). The trail going right joins up with Mercy Trail (see Hike 48). The fence makes a good turn-around point.

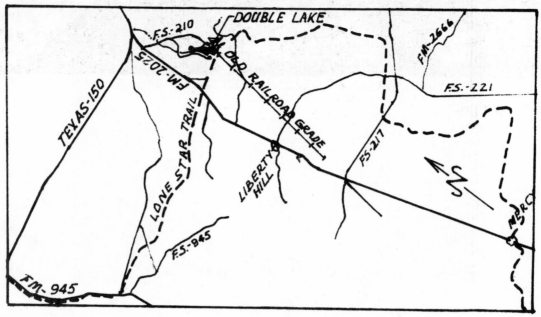

Magnolias along creek

48 MERCY TRAIL

Distance — 17.4 Miles Round Trip
Time — All Day or Backpack
Elevation Change — Little
Topographic Map — Westcott

This hike is along part of the Lone Star Trail. There are many campsites along the route which extends from Forest Service Road 217 to the old Mercy Fire Tower site on FM 2025 which is 8.7 hiking miles away. It's a very pleasant area for hiking, and you might want to add on Hike 47 (Double Lake) to make a longer backpack. If you can arrange a car shuttle, you will have a hike of less than eight hours and you will only need a day pack.

To reach the south trail head (Old Mercy Fire Tower Site), take FM 2025 north from its junction with U.S. 59 in Cleveland. About seven miles north on the right side of the road is the Old Mercy Fire Tower site and trail head. Signs mark this as a Lone Star Trail parking lot and trailhead. Aluminum triangles and rectangle signs mark the trail route. You may leave a car here for shuttle purposes at the end of the hike.

The north trailhead is about eleven miles from Cleveland where you turn right on FS 217. A Forest Service Work Center is there and a sign indicating the Big Creek Scenic Area. About a mile down FS 217 is the Lone Star Trail parking lot. The Mercy Trail proceeds South across the road from this parking lot. Aluminum signs mark the trail clearly.

A short distance from the parking lot along the trail is a sign indicating a nesting area of the endangered species, the red-cockaded woodpecker. Federal law preserves the forest from cutting around this woodpecker colony. A large stand of longleaf pine is situated in this area. Other pines along this trail include prolific loblolly and the shortleaf. Hardwoods are also well-represented and include: post oak, red oak, hickory, and magnolia. Wild grape vines drape the trees and blackberries tangle the sunny clearings. Yaupon bushes form jungles whenever foresters have allowed the sun to reach the forest floor. The red berries of the holly and the white dogwood flowers jostle for light underneath the trees. Botanists have labeled this association of plants as the true Big Thicket of Texas.

The first mile and a half is mostly on the interfluve and partly follows an old railroad tram route of the great lumber boom era (1880-1930). As the trail descends to the bottoms along Tarkington Bayou a higher and denser forest is noticeable. Tall magnolias really stand out in the forest milieu. Many campers have used the camp sites where the trail meets the creekside.

The next three miles of the trail follow the sinuous meanders of the Tarkington Bayou, a creek that is quite wet from about November to May and, dry or not, flowing most of the remainder of the year. Several gas lines and roads are crossed on this creekside hike. The animals of the dense forest include squirrels, armadillo, opossum, bobcats, water mocassins; and wood ducks have been seen nesting here. At night the call of the barred owl is common.

At about 5 miles the trail turns sharply to the southwest and away from the creek. Many choose this area as a campsite. For two miles the trail is as straight as a tram railroad line, a living memory when great sawmills at Cleveland, Fostoria, and Livingston hauled the timber of the "first forest" to the marketplace. Near 7 miles the trail turns sharp left off the tram right-of-way. It is only 1.7 miles to the old Mercy Fire Tower site which served as a fire watch from the 1930's to the 1960's. Before the fire tower was built a tall tree with ladder rungs was used to spot fires. Today, the airplane has replaced both for forest fire protection.

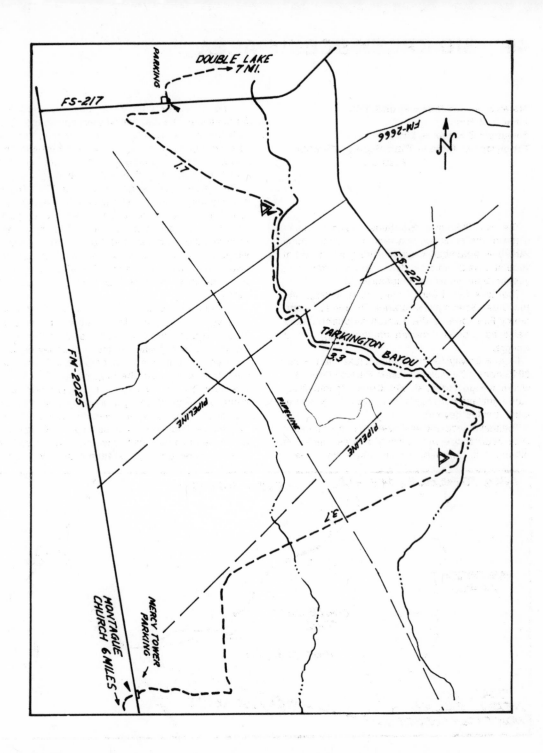

49 BIG CREEK SCENIC AREA

Distance — 2.5 Miles Round Trip
Time — 2 Hours
Elevation Change — Little
**Topographic Maps — Cold Spring, Camilla,
Westcott**

The Big Thicket of Southeast Texas contains some of the country's last remnants of a rapidly vanishing botanical kingdom. One such pocket of vegetation is being protected by the government in eastern Sam Houston National Forest.

The Lone Star Hiking Trail passes through the Big Creek Scenic Area between Double Lake and Mercy Fire Tower and a number of looped nature walks have been provided for the enjoyment of visitors.

From Highway 59 in Cleveland, take Farm Road 2025 north 10.4 miles to Forest Service Road 217 where a sign indicates Big Creek Scenic Area. Turn right, and continue to the parking area on the left 3.3 miles beyond.

The trail is wide and well used. In some places, it is in deep shade with a wash of green moss; in others, it is sun-dappled; in others, last year's magnolia leaves crunch under foot. About 350 feet from the start is a junction where you take the right fork. In the early 1900's, the Piney Woods Railroad ran through here, but the elevated roadbeds are about the only remaining evidence. A junction with the Pine Trail is 0.3 mile farther; keep right.

The route crosses and recrosses Big Creek several times. The little stream is very clear and is fed by the gradual release of underground water which is "stored" during rains. The low areas nurture little marshes and boggy areas. Ferns, winged elm, water oak, loblolly pine, American sweetgum, American beech, flowering dogwood, partridgeberry, and American holly grow in dense ranks.

At 0.4 mile beyond the Pine Trail, turn right. This puts you on the short loop trail which takes in Texas' largest magnolia — an insect-riddled, hollow veteran with a patina of moss. Just beyond the old tree, the trail veers left and soon rejoins the main trail near where the loop began.

A hundred feet to the right is a junction with White Oak Trail. Keep right. When you have come 1.5 miles, keep straight where the Double Lake Trail comes in on the right (see hike 47). Keep right at the next two trail junctions and, just before the 2.5-mile mark, turn right to return to the parking lot.

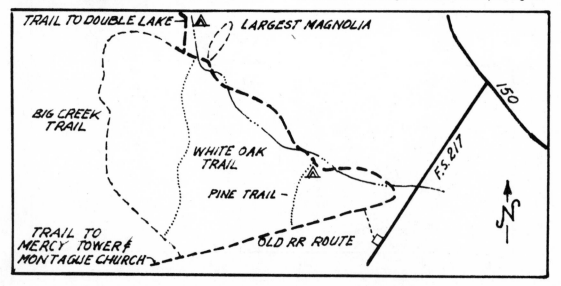

Big Creek Scenic Area

50   WINTERS BAYOU/SAN JACINTO RIVER

Distance — 6.0 Miles
Time — 2.5 Hours
Elevation Change — Very Little
Topographic Maps — Bear Creek, Westcott

This trail is the newest section of the Lone Star Hiking Trail and extends from Mercy Fire Tower (Trip 49) to Montague Church. The trail crosses the San Jacinto River and Winters Bayou, both of which can be crossed, except at times of high water, by wading or on downed trees.

Trail head parking is available at the Mercy Fire Tower, 6.5 miles northwest of Cleveland on FM 2025 and Montague Church, 1 mile west of Cleveland on highway 105 then north 5.1 miles on FM 1725.

Winters Bayou is an ecological jewel and can be reached by a 0.8 mile hike from the Montague Church trail head. From the parking lot, walk 100 yards north to the woods and northeast down a wide trail through a young pine forest to the utility right-of-way. Cross this and continue to the Bayou. On the way, view the abandoned oxbows of the stream, the giant palmettos and the climax-hardwood/pine forest.

On the southwest bank of the bayou is space for primitive camping. A side trail proceeds downstream for a few hundred yards to a magnolia grove.

The main trail goes upstream for 250 yards, crosses on a downed oak and returns downstream for 150 yards on north bank. From here proceed north for 0.3 miles through a park-like hardwood forest to an abandoned woods road. Take time out to wander through the hardwood forest to view specimens of American elm, sweetgum, wild pecan, hickory and a variety of oak. Many trees exceed 100 feet in height and some, like the elm on the trail, exceed 150 inches in diameter. From here, proceed along the trail to the palmetto plant bog, hike on to Mercy Tower (5 miles) or return to your car.

To reach Winters Bayou from the north, cross over the "Y" in the highway west of Mercy Tower site and hike through a mixed pine-hardwood forest southwest for 1.2 miles to the pipeline right-of-way. Primitive camping (no water) is available 0.2 miles south of Mercy Tower site. Turn southwest along this pipeline for 0.4 miles to the San Jacinto River. (Caution — from the south, hikers should exit the pipeline to the right at the foot of the general rise. Trail signs here are often removed or shot up by irresponsible hunters or other vandals.)

The woods on both sides of the pipeline are hardwood jungles containing abandoned oxbows and other features of floodplains. While not impenetrable, they are usually soggy and difficult to walk.

Cross the river any way you can (foot logs, wade or swim) and pick up trail on south bank at right-of-way. Walk down river to draw and proceed south along draw, cross over and walk through piney woods to tramway. FM 945 crossing is 600 yards SSW along tram. Hikers coming from south should exit tramway to the left 75 yards past fence crossing.

Cross highway and walk down trail 300 yards to abandoned oil well. Turn SE and hike along west edge of clearing and a system of abandoned woods roads past another old well site to a large trail running east to west. Go west 50 yards on the cross trail then south down a wide trail to a clearing. Cross clearing and go south along a marked system of woods trails and abandoned woods roads to another pipeline right-of-way.

Enter wide trail across pipeline, go 375 yards to cross trail (caution: when going south to north be sure to turn left at this "T"). Go WNW for 75 yards to hardwood park and south for 400 yards to clearing. Then go 100 yards SW to large palmetto plant bog. Trail skirts this bog on south and east and enters woods at SE. Go 50 yards to wide trail, left (SE) for 20 yards then south for 350 yards to Winters Bayou.

Laughing Gull

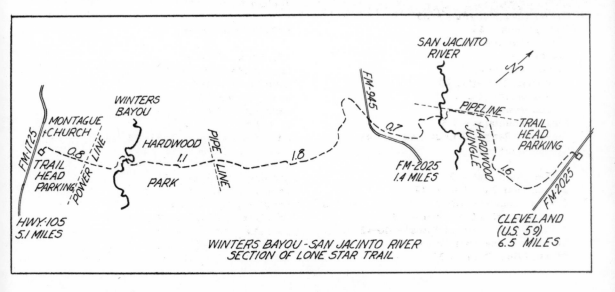

SAN JACINTO RIVER

FM-945

PIPELINE

TRAIL HEAD PARKING

0.7

WINTERS BAYOU

HARDWOOD 1.1

PIPE LINE

1.8

HARDWOOD JUNGLE

MONTAGUE CHURCH

FM-1725

.6 0.8

TRAIL HEAD PARKING

POWER LINE

PARK

FM-2025 1.4 MILES

.16

FM-2025

HWY. 105 5.1 MILES

CLEVELAND (U.S. 59) 6.5 MILES

WINTERS BAYOU - SAN JACINTO RIVER
SECTION OF LONE STAR TRAIL

INDEX TO PLACE NAMES AND HIKES

Ferns in East Texas woods